Diverting Children

from a Life

Measuring Costs

and Benefits

Peter W. Greenwood

Karyn E. Model

C. Peter Rydell

James Chiesa

Criminal Justice

Prepared for the University of California, Berkeley
and the James Irvine Foundation

RAND

Support for this effort was provided by the Crime Policy Project at the University of California, Berkeley; the James Irvine Foundation; and RAND. In particular, we want to thank University of California law professor Edward Rubin, the Crime Policy Project's director; Craig Howard, our project officer at Irvine; and Albert Williams, formerly RAND corporate research manager for the Social Policy Department, for making that support available.

We are greatly indebted to Jonathan Caulkins, associate professor of Operations Research and Public Policy at Carnegie Mellon University and codirector of RAND's Drug Policy Research Center. His review of a draft version instigated changes that sharpened the analysis and added depth to the presentation. Our RAND colleague Phyllis Ellickson provided helpful reactions to our evolving work and suggestions in making our way through the literature. Mark Moore, Guggenheim professor of Criminal Justice Policy and Management at Harvard University's Kennedy School of Public Policy, and John Reid, research director at the Oregon Social Learning Center, provided thoughtful and constructive reviews of an earlier draft.

Chapter One

INTRODUCTION

Crime has been one of the top issues on the public agenda now for a quarter century. Over the course of that period, the public response has been to progressively increase the rate at which criminals are sent to prison and the length of time they stay there. The 1980s saw the largest growth in the U.S. prison population since the penitentiary was invented, as legislatures around the country passed a flurry of new bills establishing mandatory minimum sentences for various crimes. In most states, the number of prison inmates more than tripled.

The public has ample reason to be genuinely concerned about crime. In recent years, homicide rates among juveniles have increased sharply, and homicide is now the leading cause of death among young African-American males (Reiss and Roth, 1993). And while crime rates have leveled off and have even fallen recently, there is still one violent crime reported for every 130 Americans each year.

Given the scope of the problem, it is surprising that incarceration is the only remedy evoking widespread endorsement. Incarceration's main goals are to incapacitate criminals so they can commit no further crimes for a period of time and to deter those who might contemplate criminal activity.[1] Available evidence, however, suggests that the increases in imprisonment of the past decade have not had

---

[1] Apart from its crime-reduction objectives, incarceration also serves as a punishment expressing society's sense of justice or outrage. We do not consider this objective below, since we analyze alternatives whose purpose is to prevent crime, obviating the need for punishment.

large effects on crime (Zimring and Hawkins, 1995), and the alleged deterrent effects seem particularly speculative. Nonetheless, it must be conceded that because large numbers of crimes are committed by relatively few individuals, locking up greater numbers of repeat offenders for longer periods of time should eventually have an effect. It has been estimated, for example, that California's "three-strikes" law, containing the nation's harshest and most sweeping repeat-offender sanctions, will reduce serious crimes perpetrated by adults some 28 percent if it is fully implemented (Greenwood et al., 1994).

But would even 28 percent be enough? Would one violent crime for every 180 Americans be acceptable? Are there other implements in the public-policy toolbox that could add to the gains anticipated from increased imprisonment? In particular, are there less-expensive tools? The same analysis that predicts the big decrease in crime from "three strikes" also calculates the price tag—more than $5.5 billion a year, if the law is invoked in all eligible cases. That represents an increase in California's criminal-justice-system operating costs of more than 100 percent. The study goes on to predict, however, that the new law will not be fully implemented—and will thus not achieve the benefits projected—because it will cost so much at a time of intense funding competition from other state programs. Indeed, district attorneys are already exercising considerable discretion in applying the law.

There are, of course, alternatives to deterrence and incapacitation: Those alternatives take the form of preventive and rehabilitative approaches. In this report, we address the former.

Crime-prevention efforts can take many forms, from better security devices, gun control, and improved use of streetlights to antitruancy programs and efforts to decrease school dropout rates among high-risk youths. One of the problems with various target-hardening strategies, such as providing better locks and streetlights, is that a substantial portion of the crimes prevented at the hardened site may simply be displaced to less-protected sites; the offenders will adapt. The advantage of prevention programs that focus on the offenders themselves—at an age when they are still *potential* offenders—is that the crimes prevented are not displaced (with the notable exception of market-driven crimes like drug selling and prostitution).

This report assesses the cost-effectiveness of several crime-prevention strategies that involve early intervention in the lives of people at risk of pursuing a criminal career. Because this assessment is based on limited data, the results are subject to large uncertainties. However, in comparing the alternatives with each other and with a repeat-offender minimum-sentence incarceration approach, we find differences large enough to identify some promising alternatives for further demonstration and analysis.

This research originated in an invitation by the University of California's Crime Policy Project[1] to make a presentation at a seminar on the future of criminal-justice policy in California. The seminar, which included two other presentations, was held on May 19, 1995, in Oakland and was attended by several dozen policy analysts, legislative staff members, and criminal-justice practitioners and activists.

After the seminar, RAND and the James Irvine Foundation sponsored additional work to refine the analysis. The resulting report, a product of RAND's Criminal Justice Program, is intended for an audience similar in character to that at the seminar. Although the report focuses on California, the lessons are drawn from experience in various parts of the United States and have national implications.

---

[1]The Crime Policy Project is sponsored by two University of California elements—the California Policy Seminar (a joint initiative with the California state government) and the University of California at Berkeley Law School.

CONTENTS

FIGURES

TABLES

When queried about their concerns, Americans typically list crime near the top. FBI data on crime provide ample justification for that concern. Despite headlines about falling crime rates, this year there will still be one violent crime committed for every 130 U.S. citizens— a rate several times that in most other industrialized democracies. Yet despite the seriousness of the problem, most of the money and effort devoted to solving it are restricted to a narrow range of solutions, chief among them incarceration of persons who have already committed crimes. Much less attention has been paid to diverting youths who have not yet committed crimes from doing so.

This lopsided allocation of resources is in part quite rational. When a criminal is imprisoned, there is little doubt that crimes are being prevented by that person's incapacitation. However, programs aiming to reduce the flow of children into criminal careers are not so easily evaluated. Children who will wind up in trouble with the law cannot be identified with certainty, program participation cannot ensure against eventual criminal activity, and any positive effects can wear off. Still, some benefit from such programs should be realized. How much? And at what cost?

In this report, we make an initial attempt to answer these questions, and our findings suggest that some approaches to preventing criminal careers look promising enough to warrant more extensive demonstration. Care must be taken in generalizing from our results, because the study was limited in scope and few reliable data are available on the efficacy of the programs examined. However, we tried to compensate for these shortcomings by thoroughly analyzing the sensitivity of the results to the assumptions made about program efficacy and other factors.

We consider four different approaches to intervening early in the lives of children at some risk of eventual trouble with the law. Risk of that kind is, of course, difficult to determine, but research shows that the children of young, single, poor mothers are at greater risk of engaging in criminal activity than are others. The earliest interventions might be targeted to such families, while programs for older children could be based on their behavior. The four approaches examined are as follows:

- Home visits by child-care professionals beginning before birth and extending through the first two years of childhood, followed by four years of day care. The visits are intended to provide guidance in perinatal and infant care and ward off the likelihood of abuse or neglect, both of which are associated with troubled childhoods. Day care permits a higher family income than might be possible without it, and children seeing a higher income may find activities other than crime more attractive.

- Training for parents and therapy for families with very young school-age children who have shown aggressive behavior or otherwise begun to "act out" in school.

- Four years of cash and other incentives to induce disadvantaged high school students to graduate.

- Monitoring and supervising high-school-age youths who have already exhibited delinquent behavior.

Each of these approaches has been attempted, and Table S.1 shows the efficacies of these pilot programs in terms of reductions in arrest or rearrest rates. These reductions are likely to be smaller for larger, less-intensive programs and are also likely to decay with the passage of time, especially with respect to any effects on behavior beyond the juvenile years. Table S.1 shows hypothesized effective prevention rates taking into account these scale-up and decay penalties. Larger penalties are taken for the two earlier interventions. These have been tested less often, and their effects have more opportunity for decay before children reach a crime-prone age.

Table S.1

Program Effectiveness and Cost Parameters

Parameter	Visits and Day Care	Parent Training	Graduation Incentives	Delinquent Supervision
Pilot prevention rate (%)	50	60	70	10
Effective prevention rate for juvenile crime (%)	24	29	56	8
Effective prevention rate for adult crime (%)	9	11	50	8
Targeting ratio	2	2	3	4.5
Cost per participant (thousands of dollars)	29.4	3.0	12.5	10.0

The table shows another factor influencing ultimate program benefit—the targeting ratio, or ratio of the crime rate in the group participating in the program to that in the population as a whole. Again,
the later programs can be focused more narrowly on youths at risk of
criminal activity. Finally, the table shows an estimate of the costs of
each program per participant.

When combined with other information on crime rates and criminal
careers, the data in the table permit estimates of how many serious
crimes would be averted over the lives of all program participants.
These estimates can be expressed in terms of serious crimes prevented for every million dollars spent on each program. These are
presented in Figure S.1, along with a similar estimate for one high-
profile incarceration program—California's "three-strikes" law guar-
anteeing extended sentences for repeat offenders. As the graph
shows, three of the four early-intervention approaches compare favorably in cost-effectiveness with incarceration. Some caution must
be exercised, however, before taking these numbers at face value, for
several reasons:

- The costs of the four early interventions are based solely on the
  program costs shown in the table. They do not take into account
  the savings realized by not having to eventually imprison those
  youths diverted from criminal careers. We estimated that graduation incentives would save enough money to pay most of the
  program's costs. Parent training and delinquent supervision

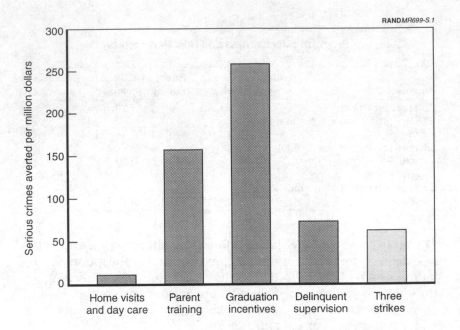

RANDMR699-S.1

**Figure S.1—Cost-Effectiveness of Early Interventions,
Compared with That of California's Three-Strikes Law**

would also save a significant portion of their costs—on the order of 20 to 40 percent.

- While three of the early interventions compare favorably to the three-strikes law in cost-effectiveness, their total impact on California's crime rate would be smaller even if implemented at full scale. A previous analysis has estimated that the three-strikes law might reduce serious crime by approximately 21 percent.[1] Graduation incentives might bring about a reduction on the order of 15 percent, the other interventions less than 10 percent.

- Because the parameter estimates shown in Table S.1 are the results of limited demonstrations, actual values could vary considerably from those shown and the results would change accord-

---

[1]See Greenwood et al., 1994. The estimate given in that study is 28 percent for adult crime, equivalent to 21 percent for all crime.

ingly. We found, however, that substantial variations in the parameter values do not result in a reversal of the cost-effectiveness outcomes relative to the three-strikes law. The star in Figure S.2, for example, shows the assumed base-efficacy rate and program cost for graduation incentives. At any combination of prevention rate and program cost below the diagonal line, graduation incentives would still be more cost-effective than the three-strikes law.

None of this suggests that incarceration is the wrong approach. The crime reductions achievable through additional incarceration—on the order of 20 percent or so—are substantial. But, with 80 percent of serious crime remaining, Americans will want to know what else can be done. This study indicates that additional crime reduction could be achieved through parent training, graduation incentives, and delinquent supervision. It might be inferred from California's vote in favor of the three-strikes law that the public believes a 21 percent reduction in crime is worth the measure's cost of $5.5 billion a year. For less than an additional billion dollars, graduation incentives and parent training could roughly double that crime reduction, if they are as effective as our analysis suggests. To find out if they are would require broader demonstration programs costing in the millions of dollars. We conclude that such demonstration programs would be an investment worth the cost.

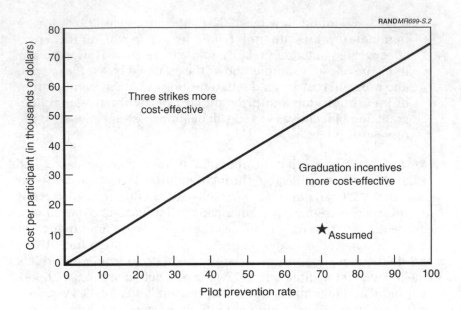

Figure S.2—How Different Combinations of Cost and Prevention Rate Influence Relative Cost-Effectiveness

Public discussions of violence-prevention programs usually emphasize those targeting high-risk youths in the age ranges where violence
is most prevalent, around 15 to 20 years of age. This was true, for example, of the debate on the 1994 federal crime bill. Many of these
programs emphasize dispute-resolution skills, mentoring, after-
school activities, and reducing the number of weapons on school
campuses, all of which are hoped to reduce the immediate likelihood
of violence among youth. Unfortunately, despite a number of recent
programs designed to demonstrate the value of such activities, their
value in reducing violence remains a matter of speculation or faith
rather than an empirically demonstrated fact (Reiss and Roth, 1993;
Tolan and Guerra, 1994).

Programs targeting the family or home situation and younger children have shown more promising results. Home-visit programs, targeting young, single, poor mothers, and enriched preschool programs that target the young children of such mothers have both been
demonstrated to produce substantial benefits to participating families and society in general. Programs increasing the parenting skills
of parents with troublesome children have also produced positive results (Farrington, 1994; Tolan and Guerra, 1994). So have programs
designed to provide structure, supervision, and support for young
delinquents (Davidson et al., 1990; Lipsey, 1992; Andrews et al.,
1990).

While individual pilot programs have yielded promising results, no
attempt has been made to compare the costs and effectiveness of
various early-intervention approaches with each other and with incarceration. Without such a comparison, it is understandable that
public officials have been reluctant to divert scarce crime-reduction
resources from incarceration to less-proven alternatives. After all,
money expended to keep a repeat offender in prison offers a fairly
high likelihood of preventing felonies, at least until the offender
passes his peak criminal years. But if the money is spent on incentives to graduate from high school, how much future crime will be
prevented? We take a first step toward answering that question here.
In so doing, we seek to determine whether more options may be
available to citizens and policymakers concerned about maximizing
the crime-fighting punch of each tax dollar.

We call this a first step because a definitive comparison is difficult to draw from the evaluations of early interventions completed to date. The studies have been small and scattered, and we have not been able to survey all of them. One purpose of our limited effort is to identify approaches with enough promise to merit further analysis of data in the literature and possibly further demonstration on a larger scale.

In the next chapter, we review what is currently known about the effectiveness of such interventions. In Chapter Three, we estimate the costs and benefits of programs tailored to the needs of California's youth.[2] The last chapter discusses the implications of our findings for public policy.

_____

[2]By restricting the scope of the analysis to California, we gain leverage from our prior work on that state and satisfy the study's charter (see the Preface). We have no reason to believe that the gist of our findings should not apply as well to the United States as a whole.

Chapter Two

OPPORTUNITIES FOR INTERVENTION IN DEVELOPMENT

In this chapter, we present what is known about several modes of early intervention to prevent crime:

- Early-childhood interventions for children at risk of later antisocial behavior.

- Interventions for families with children who are "acting out."

- School-based interventions, e.g., incentives to graduate.

- Interventions for troublesome youths early in delinquency.

All of these approaches depend on an ability to identify families with children at risk of future trouble with the law. Thus, before we proceed, let us review some of the factors permitting that identification.

There is a high degree of continuity between childhood conduct problems, delinquency, and later criminal behavior (Loeber and LeBlanc, 1990). The best predictor of any individual's future deviant or antisocial behavior is the amount and severity of similar behaviors in the past (Farrington, 1994). Age of onset and severity of juvenile record are two of the best predictors of adult criminality (Greenwood and Abrahamse, 1982; Blumstein et al., 1986).

Troublesome and delinquent children are more likely to come from troubled families and neighborhoods. Family factors associated with higher rates of delinquency include early childbearing, teenage pregnancy, and substance use during pregnancy (Farrington, 1994); low birth weight, other types of birth complications, and parent's criminal record or mental health problems (Brennan, Sarnoff, and

5

Volvaka, 1995); and poor parental supervision, erratic child-rearing behavior, parental disharmony, and parental rejection of the child (Loeber and Stouthamer-Loeber, 1986). Being abused or neglected as a child increases the likelihood of arrest for a violent crime by 38 percent (Widom, 1992).

Delinquency is not a problem that appears alone. Delinquent youths are also at higher-than-average risk for drug use, problems in school, dropping out of school, and teenage pregnancy (Elliott, Huizinga, and Menard, 1989; Greenwood, 1993). Research attempting to explain the likely sequence or relationship between these various behaviors now supports an interactional model in which all are interconnected, with causality flowing both ways between any two (Thornberry, 1987). Given this perspective, any intervention that reduces the incidence of one of these problem behaviors is likely to reduce the others as well. Thus, beneficial secondary effects on crime might be anticipated from interventions that have been shown to reduce drug use or teen pregnancy or to increase educational achievement.

EARLY-CHILDHOOD INTERVENTIONS FOR CHILDREN AT RISK

Most of us have an intuitive sense that the basic patterns of character and personality are laid down very early in life. Longitudinal studies have demonstrated, as suggested above, that inappropriate or inadequate parenting are among the strongest predictors of later delinquency (Loeber and Stouthamer-Loeber, 1986). How can individuals who are at risk of being ineffective parents be identified and what can be done about it?

Longitudinal studies consistently identify the following three factors as associated with such risks: poverty, single parenthood, and youthfulness. Any woman in one or more of these situations is at significantly higher risk of being an ineffective or abusive parent than one not in these situations (Farrington, 1994). Additional factors associated with later antisocial behavior on the part of the child include parental substance abuse, mental health problems, or criminality; birth complications; and child abuse and neglect (Sampson, 1995).

Given these findings, it can be argued that the community has an interest in helping any woman in one of these situations overcome potential problems that are likely to interfere with the healthy development of her child. During the past two decades, a number of experimental programs have demonstrated the value of home visits and early childhood education in reducing a range of problem behaviors (Farrington, 1994; Yoshikawa, 1994).

The Syracuse University Family Development Research Program recruited 108 deprived families to participate in an experimental intervention, which began during the third trimester of pregnancy. All of the families, which were predominantly African-American, had annual incomes under $20,000 (in 1996 dollars). The average age of the mothers was 18, and 85 percent were single heads of households. The major thrust of the intervention was to support parenting strategies that enhanced the development of children. This was done through weekly home visits followed by day care through the first five years of the children's lives. The home visitors were trained to help families resolve problems in child rearing, family relations, and community functioning.

Ten years after the intervention ended, a follow-up study of the Syracuse sample found that 6 percent of the experimental-program children had been referred to probation, compared to 22 percent of a group of matched controls.[1] Program youths also tended to express more positive feelings about themselves and to take a more active approach in dealing with personal problems. Girls who participated in the program showed greater school achievement and higher ratings by teachers. Parents of program youth placed more value on prosocial attitudes and behaviors than did the controls (Lally, Mangione, and Honig, 1988).

Another study in upstate New York randomly assigned at-risk women (young, poor, or single) experiencing their first pregnancy to one of the following four conditions: (1) sensory and developmental screening for the children at ages 12 and 24 months only, (2) condi-

---

[1]Although the studies of early intervention yield mutually reinforcing results, few provide statistical tests of the significance of the differences found or furnish enough information to allow such tests to be performed by others. In most cases, sample sizes are quite small.

tion 1 plus free transportation to regular prenatal and well-child vis-its, (3) condition 2 plus nurse home-visitation during pregnancy, or (4) condition 3 plus nurse home-visitation during child's first two years. Reports of child abuse or neglect during the first two years were substantially fewer among those receiving the postnatal home visits. Among women most at risk, 19 percent of those receiving no services (condition 1) were the subject of child abuse or neglect re-ports, versus 4 percent of those receiving the postnatal home visits (Olds et al., 1986a).

In another study, the Houston Parent-Child Development Center randomly assigned one-year-old Mexican-American children and their families, recruited from Houston barrios, to either a two-year program of biweekly home visits (first year) and four-times-a-week classes and day care (second year) or an "assessment only" condi-tion. Ratings by teachers five to eight years after the program's completion show significantly fewer acting-out and aggressive be-havior problems with program participants compared with controls (Johnson and Walker, 1987).

Larson (1980) compared the effects of various levels and timing of home visits for working-class pregnant women in Montreal. He found that early visits (prenatal through 12 months) resulted in im-proved home environments and infant accident rates less than half those of the controls. Another research team tested the efficacy of a protocol consisting of home visits for three years, an educational child-care program (years two and three), and bimonthly parent-group meetings. When this protocol was applied to groups of low-birth-weight children and their parents, the intervention group had higher cognitive scores and significantly lower behavioral problem scores than the control group (Brooks-Gunn et al., 1993).

The national Head Start program also provides an enriched educa-tion for disadvantaged youth, as well as increased access to health and social services. Head Start has been shown to increase educa-tional attainment and access to preventive health services—al-though, for African-Americans, the educational advantage decays quickly after program participation ends (Currie and Thomas, 1994).

Long-term follow-up of students at Perry Preschool (who were mostly African-Americans from disadvantaged homes) in Ypsilanti,

Michigan, found that those exposed to a two-year program of enriched preschool and weekly home visits had accumulated only half the arrests of a matched comparison group, up through age 27 (Schweinhart, Barnes, and Weikart, 1993). Earlier follow-up studies had found the Perry group to be more motivated in school, achieving better grades, and more likely to be employed at age 19.

Taken together these studies provide strong evidence that early home visits and supportive child care can bring about significant reductions in problem behaviors and increase cognitive functioning, especially for those youths most seriously at risk. The success of this "supportive child care" approach is in marked contrast to a number of early educational and cognitive-development interventions that did not produce the hoped-for gains in academic performance (Seitz, 1990).

INTERVENTIONS FOR FAMILIES WITH CHILDREN ACTING OUT

The interventions described in the previous section focus on families at risk of having problems with their children because of parental socioeconomic status, marital status, or age. We now turn to programs for families already having trouble with their children.

Gerald Patterson and his colleagues at the Oregon Social Learning Center (OSLC) have developed a program for training parents in how to monitor their child's behavior and respond with appropriate rewards and punishments. A series of small-scale evaluations have shown that the training reduces stealing and antisocial behavior over short periods of time (Patterson, Chamberlain, and Reid, 1982; Patterson, Reid, and Dishion, 1992). OSLC is currently experimenting with "Parenting Through Change," a training program for single parents and their children designed to reduce aggression, externalizing of problems, and school failure (Nancy Knutson, personal communication, December 1995).

Another type of parenting intervention, called functional family therapy (FFT), was developed and tested by Alexander and Parsons (1973) in Utah. Their approach focuses on modifying dysfunctional family communication, training family members to negotiate effectively, and setting clear rules about privileges and responsibilities. A number of evaluations have found statistically significant evidence that FFT reduces recidivism rates for delinquents by 30 to 50 percent (Barton et al., 1984).

Tremblay et al. (1991) tested a similar program on a group of Montreal boys identified as disruptive by their kindergarten teachers. The experimental program provided assistance in family management to the parents and training in social skills to the boys, who were between 7 and 9 years of age during the program. In a follow-up evaluation conducted when the boys had reached age 12, the treated youths were doing better in school and reported less involvement in delinquency than those in the randomly assigned control group (McCord et al., 1994). Hawkins, Von Cleve, and Catalano (1991) found that the combined effects of both parent and teacher training for a sample of Seattle youths, identified as disruptive upon entry into first grade, reduced teacher-determined rates of aggressiveness among white boys and self-destructive behavior among white girls but had no observable effects on African-American youth.

SCHOOL-BASED INTERVENTIONS

The recognition that problems in school or early dropout are primary risk factors for juvenile delinquency and drug use have led to the development of a wide range of interventions. These are generally intended to increase youths' attachment to school and provide them with skills for resisting invitations to participate in negative behavior from their delinquent peers. Unfortunately, many of these efforts have not been evaluated, and most of those evaluated have produced negligible impacts (Tolan and Guerra, 1994), particularly on later delinquency. One type of intervention that has shown highly favorable results, even on delinquency, is graduation incentives.

For the past four years, The Ford Foundation has sponsored a program aimed at helping disadvantaged youths graduate from high school and go on to college (Hahn, Leavitt, and Aaron, 1994; Taggart, 1995). The "Quantum Opportunity Program" offered learning, development, and service opportunities to at-risk youths[2] during their

---

[2]Minority youths from welfare-receiving families who lived within poverty neighborhoods.

four years of high-school and provided modest cash and scholarship incentives to provide short-run motivation. Graduation incentives were found to significantly increase high-school graduation and college-enrollment rates among participants. The program also had great success in reducing crime. Observed arrests for participating students were only three-tenths that of control students.[3]

INTERVENTIONS FOR TROUBLESOME YOUTHS EARLY IN DELINQUENCY

Between 30 and 40 percent of all boys growing up in urban areas in the United States will be arrested before their 18th birthday (Wolfgang and Tracy, 1982). Most of those arrested will not be arrested again. For those who are, each successive arrest will place them at a higher level of risk; after five or six arrests, they will have better than a 90 percent chance of being arrested again. Those who reach the five-arrest milestone have been labeled as chronic offenders—the 6 percent of all boys who account for more than 50 percent of all arrests (Blumstein et al., 1986; Wolfgang, Figlio and Sellin, 1972, among others). Most criminal careers begin in the juvenile years, and most chronic adult offenders have had multiple contacts with the juvenile-justice system (Blumstein et al., 1986).

Since the disposition of juvenile offenders is still supposed to be tailored to the individual needs and circumstances of each case, a wide variety of programs have been developed to meet these needs. A diverse array of programs serves those juveniles whose crimes or records are not very serious and whose family is sufficiently supportive that the youth can continue to reside in their home. These programs include probation, tracking and in-home supervision by private agencies, or programs in which a youth participates for part of the day and then returns home to sleep at night.

For those youths who must be placed out of their homes but do not represent such a risk that they must be removed from the commu-

---

[3]The results were 0.17 versus 0.58 arrest per person during his or her juvenile years (Taggart, 1995, p. 8). These are the total arrests accumulated through graduation from high school (or, for dropouts, through the time when graduation would normally have occurred).

nity, some jurisdictions provide or contract for a wide variety of group homes and other community living situations. Placements in such facilities are typically in the range of six months to two years, depending on the program and seriousness of the youth's offense. For those youths who represent a more serious risk to the community, many states provide a continuum of increasingly restrictive settings ranging from isolated wilderness camps and ranches to very secure fenced and locked facilities. Individual placement decisions are made on the basis of community safety, treatment needs, and amenability to treatment.

Some youth advocates claim that all but a handful of youths are best served by placing them in small community-based programs. Indeed, a number of studies have demonstrated that appropriate community-based interventions work considerably better than regular probation or short-term detention (Davidson et al., 1990). Others argue that community-based placements are too expensive and dangerous to the community. They advocate treating youths who commit serious crimes more like adults and keeping them in large, less-expensive training schools. Unfortunately, there is little hard evidence to resolve this dispute.

The starting point for any discussion of this issue is the Lipton, Martinson, and Wilks (1975) study of correctional treatment and the National Academy of Sciences reanalysis of that and other relevant studies (Sechrest, White, and Brown, 1979). Both reviewed extensive literature on a wide variety of rehabilitative programs ranging from individual psychotherapy to institutional imprisonment and concluded that no one method of correctional intervention could be said to be more effective than any other, which was interpreted as saying that "nothing worked." In fact, as many subsequent commentators (Palmer, 1978; Ross and Gendreau, 1980;) have pointed out, Lipton Martinson, and Wilks (1975) and the other reviewers identified a number of programs that appeared to have reduced recidivism rates significantly. Again, no particular intervention strategy was found to be consistently more effective than any other.

Some challenged this conclusion, arguing that the reviewers did not adequately distinguish between various types of programs (Gendreau and Ross, 1987). Others held that reviewers paid insufficient attention to the quality with which the intervention models were implemented (Greenwood and Zimring, 1985).

Additional insight regarding these issues was provided by a series of meta-analyses that allowed reviewers to combine results across several studies while controlling for a variety of program characteristics. The first of these, like the earlier reviews, found that many different correctional strategies and methods produced similar results with respect to recidivism (Garrett, 1985; Davidson et al., 1990). Later ones, however, found significant differences. A meta-analysis of 80 program evaluations by Andrews et al. (1990) concluded that appropriate correctional services could reduce recidivism by as much as 50 percent. Appropriate services were defined as those that target high-risk individuals; address the causes of crime, such as substance abuse or anger; and use styles and modes of treatment (e.g., cognitive and behavioral) that are matched with client needs and learning styles.

A meta-analysis of more than 400 juvenile program evaluations by Mark Lipsey (1992) found that behavioral, skill-oriented, and multimodal methods produced the largest effects, while some methods actually produced negative effects, such as deterrence programs (this includes "shock incarceration" and "scared-straight" techniques, which received considerable media publicity). Positive effects were larger in community rather than institutional settings. The mean effect of treatment in this study, in comparison to untreated control groups, was to reduce recidivism rates by 5 percentage points (recidivism rates for delinquents are typically on the order of 50 percent).

There are several differences between these last two studies—differences that favor the Lipsey analysis as the basis for predicting the potential impacts that might result from improved juvenile correctional programming. First, the Lipsey study was restricted to juvenile programs, while the Andrews study included programs treating both juveniles and adults. Second, the Lipsey study attempted to be comprehensive in considering evaluations, while the Andrews study used a small sample. Finally, the Lipsey study compared programs across a number of objective categories, while the Andrews study applied a somewhat subjective theoretical classification scheme that could have been biased by the coder's knowledge of the outcomes for individual evaluations.

But the conservative Lipsey estimates may not be the last word on the issue. Currently, Orange County, California, is experimenting with an intensive supervision and counseling program for youths who accumulate five or more arrests prior to age 18. Early analysis of pilot-program data suggests that the program may reduce juvenile recidivism by up to 50 percent (Orange County Probation Department, 1994).

Unfortunately, many of the youngest delinquents do not appear to be exposed to whatever benefits juvenile corrections programs have to offer until they are well on their way to developing a pattern of serious criminal behavior. In most jurisdictions, the juvenile system has little in the way to offer an 11- or 12-year-old delinquent youth because they are not yet seen as dangerous (Greenwood et al., 1983), but these delinquents disproportionately include the future violent criminals of their cohort.

Chapter Three

ESTIMATING THE DIRECT COSTS AND BENEFITS OF ALTERNATIVE APPROACHES

We have reviewed studies demonstrating that effective early intervention could reduce either the actual incidence of later criminal behavior or at least the risk factors (such as child abuse or behavioral problems in school) that are closely associated with future criminality. In this chapter, we estimate the direct costs and crime-reduction benefits of implementing such programs in California to address the needs of children at risk of future criminality. We consider four generic types of intervention: early-childhood home visits and day care; parent training and social-skills development for youths; programs aimed at improving the educational attainment of disadvantaged youths; and correctional interventions for young juvenile delinquents. We first discuss each of these, its costs, and potential. We then estimate the costs and benefits of providing these interventions to at-risk youths in California on a per-participant basis and compare programs based on the expected number of crimes prevented per million dollars spent.

A brief reflection on the nature of the prevention-versus-incarceration comparison may afford a better understanding of the parameters we take into account in estimating the cost-effectiveness of early-intervention strategies. It costs approximately $21,000 to keep someone in prison for a year (variable costs only, construction costs neglected).[1] That amount is likely to exceed the amount required to induce someone to stay in school, for example. But that

---

[1]Welch, Richard S., Chief, California Offender Information Services Branch, memorandum, March 14, 1994.

does not mean graduation incentives are more cost-effective than incarceration. Several other factors must be taken into account:

- Targeting. Someone who is incarcerated has been identified as a criminal, but it is not possible to identify with confidence who among a population of potential dropouts will turn to a life of crime. The number of youths who receive graduation incentives must thus be larger than the number of criminals who are imprisoned to realize the same reduction in crime.

- Efficacy. As should be clear from the previous chapter, preventing crime through one of the early interventions described here is not like preventing disease with a vaccine. Some large fraction of "treated" individuals may still go on to a life of crime. But it is all but certain that someone in a prison cell will not be able to commit more crimes.

- Decay. Even where prevention is effective, its influence may wear off after a while. Again, the effect of imprisonment is in full force for the entire span of incarceration.

- Delays. Locking someone up averts crimes immediately. A prevention program does not reduce the crime rate until its participants reach the age when they would otherwise have begun offending.

TYPES OF EARLY INTERVENTION: COSTS AND POTENTIAL

To calculate costs and potential benefits for each type of intervention, we use what we know from the literature and elsewhere to determine the values of program parameters. Explicitly, we must answer the following questions:

- What percentage of the population is to be treated, and how much crime do they commit?

- What is the cost per treatment?

- How effective is each program at preventing crime?

- How will effectiveness change if the program is expanded?

- How long do effects persist after treatment has ceased?

Working from the answers to these questions, we calculate the impact of each program on crime and criminal-justice spending. To do so, we rely on a mathematical model of criminal populations in prison and on the street, as affected by criminal career initiation, arrest and sentencing, release, and desistance from criminal activity. This model was developed for RAND's analysis of California's three-strikes law (Greenwood et al., 1994), and at the end of this chapter we compare the effects of the prevention strategies with those of the three-strikes law. Details of the calculations are in Appendix A.

Population Treated and Crime Committed

Nationally, about one out of four children lives in a household whose income is below the poverty line (Carnegie Corporation, 1994). We know that nationwide, there is no father present or willing to provide any kind of economic support for about 30 percent of all births. This fraction is probably somewhat higher in California's as a whole, and certainly much higher in California's inner cities. Finally, about 12 percent of births in California are to teenage mothers. We thus conservatively estimate that about one-quarter of California's children come from families having one or more of the characteristics identified above that place them "at risk" for eventual involvement in violent behavior. This amounts to 150,000 of the 600,000 children born in California every year (according to 1990 data).

We assume that early-home-visit/day-care and parent-training interventions would be appropriate for the entire population of at-risk youths. Indeed, most home-visit/day-care interventions target children from "disadvantaged backgrounds" (see Schweinhart, Barnes, and Weikart, 1993; Lally, Mangione, and Honig, 1988), which may be characterized quite similarly to what we consider as at risk. It would be ideal to treat only those individuals who will eventually become offenders, but this is unknowable at the age when the intervention is undertaken. However, both graduation incentives and delinquent supervision target youths who are already in trouble: those with poor school performance, arrests, drug use, etc. Eligibility for these programs could thus be based on criteria more specific to the likelihood of future violence than earlier interventions, so the former could be targeted to fewer youths. We thus assume that home-visit/day-care and parent-training programs would be applicable to

25 percent of the population, while graduation incentives and delinquent supervision apply to only 10 percent and 5 percent of youths, respectively.

A narrower definition for treatment eligibility should also be associated with a treated population that commits a large number of crimes relative to the general population. To this end, we developed the concept of a "targeting ratio," which is the number of crimes per person in the population targeted by the program (assuming no treatment) versus that per person in the general population. A targeting ratio of 1.0 indicates a participant group that commits crimes at the same rate as persons in the rest of the population. Targeting ratios greater than 1.0 indicate groups with greater criminal activity than the remainder of the population.

Programs that begin at earlier ages are expected to have a lower targeting ratio since it is difficult to predict at that age who will become a high-rate offender. However, among the interventions considered here, information on preintervention criminality for treatment and control groups is available only for graduation incentives, where the ratio was 3 (i.e., persons in the targeted population, if untreated, commit 3 times as many crimes as those in the population as a whole).[2] We use this as a benchmark. We chose a targeting ratio of 2 for home-visit/day-care and parent-training programs, to reflect the fact that younger children cannot be targeted as effectively. We chose a ratio of 4.5 for delinquent supervision since those youths are already heavily involved with the juvenile-justice system at the time of treatment.

Program Cost

According to the studies reviewed in the previous chapter, a generic early-home-visit/day-care program designed to reduce the incidence of child abuse, neglect, and delinquent behavior would include two primary core elements: weekly home visits beginning by the third trimester of pregnancy and running through the child's second year, and full-time day care and education from ages two through five. We assume a cost of $2,700 per child for each year of home visitation,

---

[2]Derivation of this is in Table A.4.

which is the annual cost in 1995 dollars of prenatal and nurse home visits in the upstate New York study by Olds et al. (1986). We use a figure of $6,000 per year for average annual day care and early-child-hood education, based on the average of costs for the Perry Preschool program (Schweinhart, Barnes, and Weikart, 1993) and the National Head Start initiative (Head Start Bureau, 1995).[3]

The typical parent-training program involves between 10 and 20 sessions of instruction and one-on-one counseling and coaching (Patterson, Reid, and Dishion, 1992). We use a figure of $500 per family from the Oregon Divorce Study for instruction and supplies. We add to that $2,500 per family to cover program management and administration (borrowed from the detailed cost data on the Perry Preschool program, which we assume would have similar adminis-trative costs), for a total of $3,000 per family.

Data on the costs of graduation incentives are readily available. The cost of this program is $3,130 per youth, for each of four years of high school. This includes the cost of program staff, student materials and incentives, and space and equipment rental.[4]

There is little information available on the costs of programs for young delinquents. Very few programs exist, and most are built into other systems and cannot be costed out. The Orange County Probation Community Action Association's "8%" program men-tioned above costs about $5,000 per youth. It obtains many supplies and services, however, through donation and transfers. We were told that donated and in-kind receipts are about equal to those paid for with program-specific funds (Kurz, Gwen, Orange County Probation Dept., personal communication, December 1, 1995). We thus use a figure of $10,000 per youth for participation in a fully funded delin-

---

[3]We did not attempt an exhaustive appraisal, and we may well have omitted some items from our costing, both for this intervention and for those that follow. However, we believe we have accounted for the bulk of program costs, and we report below the results of a sensitivity analysis showing that, in some cases, costs must be substantially off if the outcome is to be reversed.

[4]The reported cost of program staff, student materials, and incentives was $10,600 per participant over the four program years (Taggart, 1995, p. 7). In this analysis, we add $1,920 per participant ($1,000 per month for a 25-student group) to cover space and office equipment that were donated in The Ford Foundation experiment but would have to be paid for under full implementation.

quent-supervision program. Table 1 summarizes the costs for all of these programs.

Effectiveness at Reducing Crime

For this exploratory report, we did not endeavor to conduct an exhaustive review of the existing literature on early interventions. We compiled the results of a number of existing studies and attempted to learn what we could from this limited sample. Thus, our best guess for program effectiveness is based only on the research we considered. Furthermore, the studies we surveyed report results in a variety of terms—arrests, rearrests, referrals to probation, self-reported activity, and teacher and parent evaluations. We assume a roughly linear relationship between the outcome variables measured and future serious crimes committed. Even in the studies we relied on most heavily—those reporting arrests and rearrests—links of these variables to rates of serious crime are not self-evident and may indeed be quite complex. But because we aimed for suggestive rather than definitive results, we believed the assumption of a linear relationship would be satisfactory.[5] Table 2 shows our assumed values for pilot-program effectiveness. (See Appendix A for the literature survey.)

Table 1

Annual Program Costs

Program Cost	Home Visit/ Day Care	Parent Training	Graduation Incentives	Delinquent Supervision
Year 1	$2,700	$3,000	$3,130	$10,000
Year 2	$2,700		$3,130	
Year 3	$6,000		$3,130	
Year 4	$6,000		$3,130	
Year 5	$6,000			
Year 6	$6,000			
Total	$29,400	$3,000	$12,520	$10,000

[5]As with costs, the sensitivity analysis at the end of this chapter indicates that our assumed prevention rates can in some cases be varied substantially without reversing the outcome.

Table 2

Program Effectiveness and Targeting Ratio

Assumption	Home Visit/ Day Care	Parent Training	Graduation Incentives	Delinquent Supervision
Pilot prevention rate:				
Percentage of treatment-group crime prevented by pilot program	50	60	70	10
Modifiers of pilot prevention rate:				
Percentage penalty due to scale-up	40	40	20	15
Additional percentage decay for juvenile crime	20	20	0	0
Additional percentage decay for adult crime	70	70	10	5
Effective prevention rate for juvenile crime	24	29	56	8
Effective prevention rate for adult crime	9	11	50	8
Targeting ratio	2	2	3	4.5

We also considered that most evaluations for which prevention rates were available were small, intensive pilot programs, which are likely to be more effective than large-scale, expanded programs. We thus include a modifying parameter to account for the effect of scale-up on program efficacy. The values chosen for this parameter reflect the relative size of each program, i.e., the larger the percentage of a cohort treatable by a program, the larger the expected penalty due to scale-up. We chose a scale-up penalty of 40 percent for early-home-visit/day-care and parent-training programs, and 20 percent and 15 percent for graduation incentives and delinquent supervision, respectively.

Most evaluations also have follow-up periods that are too brief to assess long-term program benefits. Indeed, some studies have shown that positive program effects decay rapidly after program completion (Ellickson and Bell, 1990; Currie and Thomas, 1994). We thus incorporated another parameter to account for decay in effectiveness due to time. We allowed time-decay to affect juvenile and adult crimes differently since different programs are administered at different ages. We assumed that graduation incentives and delinquent supervision do not decay in their effectiveness on juvenile crimes, since they are administered during adolescence. At the other extreme, we attached large decay rates to prevention of adult crimes by home-visit/day-care and parent-training programs since they are administered at a very early age (in some cases, beginning before birth). The values chosen for this parameter are also presented in Table 1. (Later in the analysis, we also discuss how sensitive cost-effectiveness is to changes in pilot-program efficacy and the various decay rates.)

To estimate the eventual effectiveness of a scaled-up program, then, we multiply the pilot prevention rate by 100 percent minus the scale-up penalty and by 100 percent minus the decay rate for either juvenile or adult crime. Thus, the effective prevention rate of a scaled-up home-visit/day-care program against juvenile crime is estimated as

$$50\% \times (100\% - 40\%) \times (100\% - 20\%) = 50\% \times 60\% \times 80\% = 24\%.$$

The effective prevention rates against juvenile and adult crime are given in Table 2.

COMPARING COSTS, BENEFITS, AND COST-EFFECTIVENESS

We calculate cost-effectiveness for the treated cohort. That is, we consider the costs of delivering a set of services to at-risk youth or their families beginning in the current year and the eventual benefits in terms of crimes prevented over time for that group of youths. We take this cohort approach instead of considering the drop in the overall crime rate over some period of time because that rate includes crimes committed by criminals too old to be eligible for the interventions.

As shown in Table 1, two of the programs last only a year. For the others, program costs accumulate beginning in the first year and accrue for the duration of the intervention. We discount future costs at an annual rate of 4 percent to reflect the lower present value of future dollars.[6] Discounted costs are then summed over all program years to determine the net present value of total program cost per participant.

We estimate program effectiveness, i.e., benefits, in terms of the number of serious crimes[7] prevented *per program participant.*[8] To derive this, we apply the percentages in the above section to the number of serious crimes that an *average* program participant would be expected to commit in a lifetime. That is derived from the number of crimes expected in the whole cohort's "lifetime" and the percentage of the cohort's crime that the treated group is responsible for. In steady state, the number of serious crimes for one cohort across all calendar years would equal the number of serious crimes committed in a given year across all cohorts.[9] From FBI data and national surveys, we know the latter number, including crimes not reported to the police, approached 1,200,000 in California for 1994 (extrapolated from U.S. Department of Justice, 1992). The treated group's percentage of cohort crime is derived from the targeting ratio specific to the intervention. Appendix B contains detailed tables showing this series of calculations.

Since these interventions are conducted at young ages, benefits may greatly lag costs, as in the case of early home visits and day care, so we consider benefits accumulated over a 30-year period from the on-

[6]A $5,000 cost incurred now is a bigger cost than $5,000 incurred next year because the latter will be partially offset by the interest it earns in the meantime. Discounting is a standard practice in the economic analysis of social programs.

[7]Serious crimes recognized by California Penal Code Section 1192.7 include homicide, rape, arson, robbery, aggravated assault, and residential burglary. It should be kept in mind that the last three categories account for some 80 percent of serious crimes.

[8]We do not mean to imply that all program participants would have committed crimes in the absence of the program or that the program works by reducing by the same amount the number of crimes each participant would have committed. For ease of accounting, we speak of an average participant. The manner in which crimes are actually distributed across participants does not bear on the results we obtain.

[9]We make the steady-state assumption to simplify the analysis. In fact, California's population is not in steady state and will not be at any time in the foreseeable future. The population and thus the number of crimes is increasing. The current cohort is larger than the average-sized cohort contributing to California's current crime rate, so the current cohort should commit more than 1,174,000 serious crimes. As a result, all our benefit estimates are conservative (since more crimes will be prevented by a given intervention) and our calculated costs per crime prevented are generous.

set of the intervention.[10] We distribute the anticipated lifetime number of crimes prevented over a period running from age 14 through year 30 following intervention onset.[11] We assume the number of crimes prevented in any year to be 10 percent smaller than that in the previous year. This "tilts" crimes toward the earlier years, reflecting an estimated 10 percent per year desistance rate among criminals (that is, every year, 10 percent of criminals cease being criminals; see Greenwood, et al., 1994, p. 55). We then apply a 4 percent cumulative discount rate to calculate the net present value of crime-prevention benefits.[12]

The benefits, costs, and cost-benefit and benefit-cost ratios for each of the alternatives are presented in Table 3. Detailed, year-by-year results are given in Appendix A, which also details the mechanics of calculating cost-effectiveness.

The net present values of costs per participant follow fairly closely the undiscounted values from Table 1. None of the interventions lasts very far into the future, so discounting does not greatly reduce any of the costs.

The differences among program benefits—serious crimes prevented—depend on the differences among program effectiveness values and targeting ratios from Table 2. Our high estimates of benefits for graduation incentives are based principally on an ultimate projected effectiveness rate several times those of the other interventions. This higher rate is largely due to modest anticipated penalties for scaling up the program and for decay of effectiveness with the passage of time. The projected benefits of the other three

---

[10]This is essentially equivalent to a lifetime of crime prevention, as criminal careers typically end within 30 years of the ages at which childhood interventions begin.

[11]For the two adolescent interventions, this is a 30-year period. For interventions beginning before age 14, it is less than 30 years: 25 in the case of parent training and 17 for home visits and day care.

[12]Discounting is applied to both costs and effects to ensure consistent time preference among plans. The necessity of this is discussed in detail in Keeler and Cretin (1983) and is used similarly in Rydell and Everingham (1994). Intuitively, one would presumably pay more now to avert a crime to be committed now than to avert one to be committed several years from now. Note that condensing criminal careers for the two earlier interventions (see preceding footnote) has the effect of slightly overestimating the net present value of the crimes those interventions avert.

Table 3

Cost-Effectiveness of Early Interventions After 30 Years

	Home Visit/ Day Care	Parent Training	Graduation Incentives	Delinquent Supervision
Cost per participant	$29,400	$3,000	$12,520	$10,000
NPV[a] of cost per participant	$26,290	$3,000	$11,816	$10,000
Serious crimes prevented per participant	0.59	0.71	4.16	0.99
NPV of serious crimes prevented per participant	0.30	0.47	3.05	0.72
Dollars per serious crime prevented	$89,035	$6,351	$3,881	$13,899
Serious crimes prevented per million dollars spent	11	157	258	72

[a]Net present value.

programs are not so far apart from each other. Delinquent supervision is the strongest of those three because it is administered late enough to target a relatively high-risk set of youths; early home visits and day care are the weakest because of the delay in realizing their effects.

Since graduation incentives are by far the most effective of the interventions and are not terribly costly, they turn out to be the most cost-effective. Parent training comes in second, largely because it is so inexpensive. Early home visits and day care are the least effective and most costly of the interventions and thus have the least favorable cost-benefit and benefit-cost ratios.

Comparison of Early Intervention with Incarceration

We have now reviewed evidence bearing on the effectiveness of early-intervention strategies in reducing later criminality and used that information to estimate the costs and crime-reduction benefits of four particular strategies. Here we discuss the relative cost-effectiveness of these strategies, in comparison with long mandatory sentences, and the implications of these findings for public policy.

Greenwood et al. (1994) estimates that the California three-strikes law, if applied in all eligible cases, would reduce the number of serious felonies committed by adults in any one year by approximately 28 percent (or 329,000 crimes). They also estimate that such application would cost an additional $5.5 billion a year in additional criminal-justice funding, primarily reflected in the costs of constructing and operating additional prison facilities. That works out to $16,000 per serious felony prevented. Other, more selective extended-sentencing policies were examined, but even with the best of these, the cost per serious crime prevented would still be about $12,000. These estimates were derived from the mathematical model mentioned near the beginning of this chapter.

Since we have analyzed the cost-effectiveness of early interventions in the same units as that for California's three-strikes law, we can now compare programs. Figure 1 graphs each early-intervention

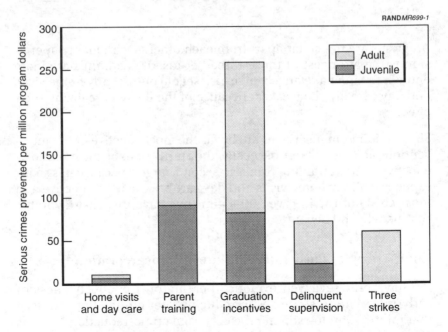

Figure 1—Serious Crimes Prevented per Million Dollars

program and California's three strikes in terms of crimes prevented per million dollars.

As the figure shows, two of the four early interventions considered should be more cost-effective at reducing serious crime than California's three-strikes law. A third intervention should be roughly equivalent. However, four major caveats need to be kept in mind when considering the results presented in this graph.

First, the benefits and costs we have presented so far for the early interventions have been restricted to crimes averted and costs for program operation. They do not include the reduction in prison operating and other criminal-justice system costs associated with the crime reduction. These costs are particularly important in a comparison with the three-strikes law, which achieves its crime-reduction benefits through *additions* to criminal-justice-system costs. Figure 2 illustrates the criminal-justice-system savings achieved through early intervention, as estimated by the same mathematical model used to

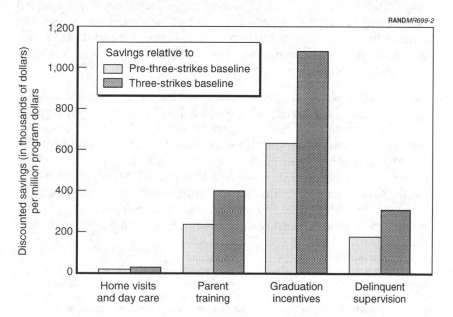

Figure 2—Criminal Justice System Savings from Some Early
Interventions Are a Substantial Fraction of Program Costs

estimate the costs and benefits of the three-strikes law. As we did with the crime-reduction benefits in Figure 1, we present savings per million dollars of program cost. Savings are presented relative to costs that would have been incurred under sentencing laws extant prior to three strikes and relative to the new three-strikes regime. We show both because true savings are likely to fall somewhere between the two.[13] The model's estimates of three-strikes costs assume application to all eligible cases, and, as mentioned above, universal application is unlikely to transpire.

As shown in the figure, a million dollars spent on graduation incentives should result in a savings to the criminal-justice system of $600,000 to $1.1 million. In other words, over the long term the program would probably save enough money to pay most of its costs. Criminal-justice-system savings would pay about a third of the costs of parent training and about a quarter of the costs of delinquent supervision.

Other costs will also accrue. For example, some individuals rescued from criminal careers by early intervention will need social-services support in the form of publicly provided health care and other welfare programs. Of course, others will work and pay taxes, providing additional cost offsets.

The second caveat is that the criterion used for the comparisons in Figure 1 does not satisfy all criminal-justice policymaker goals. Crimes prevented per dollar of program cost is just one important evaluation criterion; another is total crimes prevented. A highly cost-effective approach that could prevent only a tiny portion of the state's crime might not be viewed as very useful. Another useful criterion, particularly in a constrained-budget environment, might be total cost. In Table 4, we show total cost and crime prevented for the three-strikes law, assuming application to all eligible cases,[14] and

---

[13]Clearly, more savings are achieved relative to three strikes than to the preceding sentencing regime. But that is not the point of the graph. The savings differential is due to the higher cost of the new sentences, but those costs support crime-reduction benefits. Crime-reduction benefits relative to program-operating costs are shown in Figure 1.

[14]Greenwood et al. (1994) predict that the three-strikes law will bring about a 27.7 percent reduction in serious crime committed by adults. Because juveniles commit

Table 4

Total Benefits and Costs from Program Alternatives
at Full Scale Across California

	Three Strikes	Home Visits/ Day Care	Parent Training	Graduation Incentives	Delinquent Supervision
Percentage of cohort treated	NA[a]	25	25	10	5
Total benefit (% serious crime reduction)	21.4	2.7	4.4	11.4	1.3
Total program cost (millions of dollars per year)	5,520	3155	360	570	240

NOTE: Benefits and costs are discounted.

[a]Not applicable (three strikes not implemented on cohort basis).

for each of the early interventions, assuming application as given above (under "Population Treated and Crime Committed" and repeated in the table's first row).

In Figure 3, we plot the projected benefits of the three-strikes law and the early-intervention alternatives at full scale against total program costs. The most favorable position in this graph is to the upper left—high benefit, low cost. As is evident from the figure, while the early-intervention alternatives would be much less costly than the three-strikes law, none of them would come close to matching the total impact of the law. However, graduation incentives do provide most of the benefit at about one-tenth the cost.[15]

The third caveat is that these results cannot be generalized to other incarceration alternatives. California's three-strikes law is notably

---

22.7 percent of serious crimes, the Greenwood et al. estimate is the equivalent of a 21.4 percent reduction in all serious crime, which is the number shown in the table.

[15]The total benefits shown are dependent on the percentage of the cohort treated, which is consistent with that in the cost-benefit analysis above. Any of the interventions could be expanded somewhat to achieve a larger total impact on crime by treating a greater percentage of the cohort. Cost would also go up, and cost-effectiveness would come down. However, for parent training and graduation incentives, some increase in impact might be achieved at a benefit-cost ratio that is still greater than that of the three-strikes law.

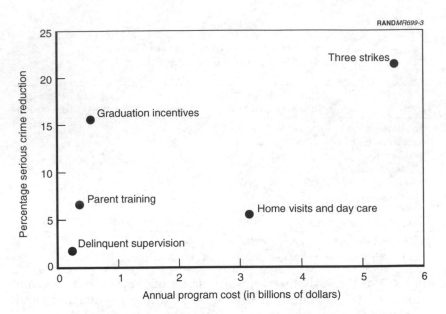

Figure 3—Early-Intervention Alternatives Would Be Much Less Costly
but Have Less Impact on Crime Than the Three-Strikes Law

inefficient because the breadth of applicability of third-strike life
sentences ensures that many will be given to criminals who do not
commit serious crimes at high rates.[16]   Other jurisdictions, e.g.,
Washington State, have passed three-strike laws more narrowly
focused on violent criminals than California's. However, while these
laws might be more cost-effective than California's, their narrow focus is likely to limit their total impact on crime.

Finally, as we have mentioned, there is considerable uncertainty associated with the data on which the crime-reduction benefits are
based. In the next subsection, we try to quantify the implications of
that uncertainty for the cost-benefit comparisons.

---

[16]This is not to say that such sentences are undeserved. We are making an observa-
tion based on efficiency, not justice.

Sensitivity to Parameter Assumptions

To quantify the implications of uncertain parameter values, we varied those values to determine the effects. Specifically, we used threshold analysis, which permits identification of parameter changes necessary to reverse the direction of the results. Here, we identify the parameter changes necessary for California's three-strikes law to become as cost-effective as early intervention.[17] We concentrate here on the two early interventions that are most likely to be more cost-effective than California's three-strikes law: parent training and graduation incentives.

First, we examined one-way thresholds, i.e., the threshold value for each parameter while holding equal *all other* parameter values (see Table 5). One-way threshold values were calculated for each variable by using values for the other parameters from Table 2. Analysis of these thresholds suggests that the cost-effectiveness of these early interventions relative to the three-strikes law is quite insensitive to variations in one parameter at a time. The threshold targeting ratios for parent training and graduation incentives were 0.4 and 0.7, respectively. That is, the targeting ratio for parent training has to drop to 0.4 before the three-strikes law becomes as cost-effective. Recall that the targeting ratio is the ratio of crimes committed in the target population to those committed in the whole population. Thus, populations targeted for early intervention could be *less* at risk of criminal careers than the population as a whole and early interventions would still be more cost-effective than the three-strikes law.

The thresholds on pilot prevention rate were 12 percent and 17 percent for parent training and graduation incentives. That is, the pilot prevention rates (and ultimate prevention rates) would need to be less than a third of those shown in Table 2 for these early interventions to be less cost-effective than the three-strikes law. Among the thresholds on modifying assumptions, those on additional decay for adult crimes are the most striking. Even at 100 percent for both parent training and graduation incentives, these decay rates cannot reverse the cost-effectiveness results. That is, these programs are more cost-effective even if their effects only last through the years of ju-

---

[17]We hold constant the parameters generating the three-strikes cost-effectiveness results; however, they are also uncertain.

Table 5

Sensitivity of Assumptions—Threshold Parameter Values Beyond Which Three Strikes Is More Cost-Effective Than Early Intervention

Assumption	Home Visits and Day Care	Parent Training	Graduation Incentives	Delinquent Supervision
Cost per person treated (1993$)	>$5,413	>7,744	>52,885	>$11,795
Targeting ratio:				
Crime per person in treatment group vs. crime in population cohort	<10.9	<0.4	<0.7	<3.8
Pilot prevention rate:				
Percentage of treatment-group crime prevented	NA	<12%	<17%	<8%
Modifiers of pilot prevention rate:				
Percentage decay due to scale-up	NA	>88%	>81%	>28%
Additional percentage decay for adults	NA	>113%	>111%	>26%
Additional percentage decay for juveniles	NA	>69%	>76%	>15%
Discount rate	NA	>16%	>100%	>7%

NOTES: NA indicates not applicable—the analysis results in values less than zero. ">" indicates that the parameter must be greater than the threshold, while "<" indicates that the parameter must be less than the threshold for three strikes to be more cost-effective than early intervention. Parameter values assumed in the analysis are given in Tables 1 and 2, except for discount rate, which was 4 percent. No analysis was run for percentage of cohort treatable by a program, because that affects cost-effectiveness only through the targeting ratio.

venile crime. Note that the findings are not sensitive to plausible changes in discount rate, for which conventionally assumed values are 5 percent or less.[18] The full set of threshold values for all variable parameters appears in Appendix B.

We also conducted a two-way threshold analysis in which we varied both pilot prevention rate and program cost. The analysis for parent training is shown in Figure 4. The star indicates our assumed pilot

---

[18]In running the sensitivity analysis for the discount rate, we adjusted only the early-intervention rate, not the three-strikes rate. Adjusting the latter would have little effect on the outcome, because the profiles of costs and benefits for the three-strikes law do not vary greatly.

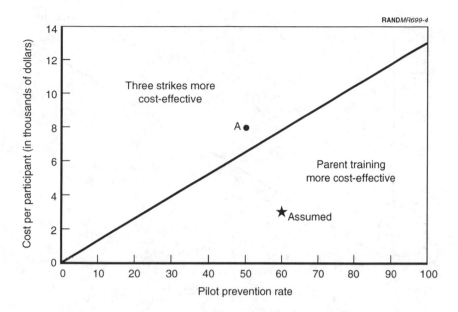

**Figure 4—Threshold Values of Program Cost and Pilot Prevention
Rate, Where Parent Training Becomes More Cost-Effective
Than Three Strikes**

prevention rate and program cost. For every combination of prevention rate and program cost lying below the diagonal line, parent
training is more cost-effective than the three-strikes law. For every
combination above the diagonal, three strikes is more cost-effective.
Thus, if the discounted value of parent-training program costs
turned out to be $8,000 instead of our projected $3,000, and if the
pilot prevention rate were 50 percent instead of 60 (point A in Figure
4), three-strikes would be more cost-effective. The same analysis is
depicted for graduation incentives and delinquent supervision in
Figures 5 and 6 (note that vertical scales differ). Here, we do not
consider early-childhood interventions since the parameter values
required for cost-effectiveness greater than three strikes are impos-
sible to achieve (e.g., having to prevent more than 100 percent of an
individual's crimes).

The threshold graphs reflect the variation among the early-intervention alternatives in their cost-effectiveness relative to the three-

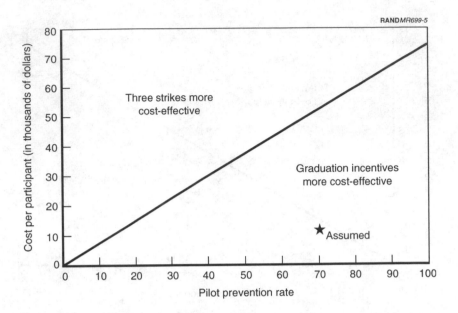

**Figure 5—Threshold Values of Program Cost and Pilot Prevention
Rate, Where Graduation Incentives Become More
Cost-Effective Than Three Strikes**

strikes law. The closer the star is to the diagonal, the smaller the
parameter change required for three strikes to surpass the cost-effectiveness of the early intervention. As expected, these points are relatively far from the threshold line for parent training and graduation
incentives since these programs are quite cost-effective relative to
three strikes under our parameter assumptions. The point is much
closer to the line for delinquent supervision since this program is
only marginally more cost-effective under our assumptions. Thus,
only a small change in parameter values would be necessary for
delinquent supervision to be less cost-effective than the three-strikes
law. Since such changes are well within our uncertainties, we do not
conclude that the delinquent supervision is more cost-effective than
the three-strikes law. However, for graduation incentives, our assumed prevention rate would have to be 25 percent too high *and* our
cost off by a factor of 3 for three strikes to be more cost-effective. It
therefore seems prudent to conclude that it is not likely to be so.

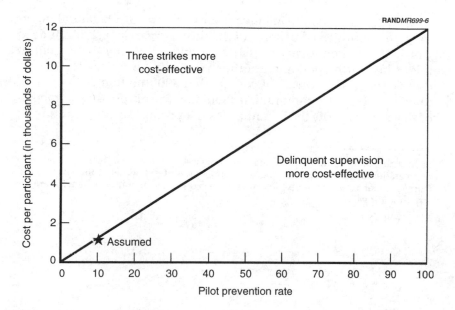

Figure 6—Threshold Values of Program Cost and Pilot Prevention
Rate, Where Delinquent Supervision Becomes More
Cost-Effective Than Three Strikes

Final Observations

Our analysis indicates that two early-intervention alternatives appear
to be more cost-effective than one high-profile, widely endorsed incarceration alternative—California's three-strikes law. We have already made the point that these results cannot be generalized to all
other incarceration alternatives. Neither should it be inferred from
our results that California's three-strikes law is a bad deal for the
state. No analysis can confidently demonstrate that the law's projected 21 percent reduction in crime is not worth its $5.5 billion-per-
year cost. In fact, it might be inferred from the initiative's over-
whelming approval by California voters that the state's citizens think
the benefits are worth the cost.

But it is worth noting that, at least according to this preliminary analysis, the graduation incentives and parent-training interventions
could together reduce serious crime by 22 percent at a combined an-

nual cost of less than $1 billion. That would be a substantial increment to the projected benefits of the three-strikes law. If it is indeed worth $5.5 billion a year to reduce serious crime by 21 percent, it might be worth spending another $900 million a year to roughly double that reduction.[19] Of course, that $900-million figure is very uncertain, but, at a minimum, it should be worth spending a fraction of that sum to verify the potential of such promising interventions.

---

[19]Because parent training would make it unnecessary for some of its beneficiaries to need graduation incentives, and because both early interventions would divert youth from criminal careers and the consequent strike-related sanctions, the benefits are not strictly additive.

Chapter Four

CONCLUSIONS AND POLICY IMPLICATIONS

The early-intervention approaches described earlier in this report offer an alternative means of reducing serious crime. The rough estimates of benefits and costs offered here suggest that three of the four compare favorably with a high-profile incarceration alternative (California's three-strikes law) in terms of serious crime averted per dollar expended. If implemented on a large scale, at least one of the alternatives might have a total impact on crime that could add substantially to the anticipated effect of mandatory repeat-offender sanctions in the penal code.

Of the early interventions examined, graduation incentives for high-risk youths (as used in the Quantum Program) appear to hold the most promise. Our preliminary analysis suggests that the cost of preventing serious crimes with this program is somewhere around $4,000 per crime (or around 250 serious crimes prevented per million program dollars). This takes into account the graduation incentives' discounting advantage: In contrast to parent training, results from a well-designed graduation incentive program will begin to be felt within just a few years after the program is implemented, because the targeted youth are very close to their most crime-prone years.

The parent-training intervention could be relatively cost-effective over the long run at a cost of some $6,500 per serious felony prevented (160 serious crimes averted per million dollars spent). For this intervention, there is no significant crime prevention effect during the first five years after initial implementation because youths are usually in the seven-to-ten-year age range when this intervention is administered and require another five years or so before their disruptive behavior might result in serious crimes. Of course, these cal-culations assume that a large number of parents would be willing to participate in parent-training programs, an assumption that cannot be validated without some careful testing. A number of experimental programs have encountered difficulties enrolling parents of high-risk youth (Kumfer and Turner, 1990–1991).

The cost per serious crime prevented for both of these first two inter-ventions is much lower than that for the three-strikes law. In fact, even if the crime-prevention rates of these programs are only a third of what we have assumed, they will still be much more effective than three strikes. We also estimate that the two programs, if imple-mented at full scale, could add substantially to the total reduction in crime predicted to occur as a result of the three-strikes law.

Another cost-effective intervention is delinquent supervision at a cost of around $14,000 per serious crime prevented (about 70 serious crimes prevented per million dollars). This cost assumes that the short-term reductions in recidivism observed for such programs hold up over time. It appears to be slightly lower than the analogous cost for the three-strikes law because it is directed at the start, rather than the end, of the criminal career for a very high-risk group. We assume society attaches a higher value to preventing a crime in the near future than to preventing one later. Here, the impacts are felt almost immediately, because the intervention comes shortly before the peak ages of criminal behavior—16 to 20 years of age.

The early home-visit and day-care intervention works with high-risk youths and their families during the first five years of childhood. This intervention requires very large expenditures to affect large numbers of youths. Since youths do not begin to commit serious crimes until their early teenage years, there is almost a 15-year delay between when the intervention is applied and when it begins affecting serious street crimes. The high costs per crime prevented for early home visits and day care result from the intervention's expense ($29,400 per child over the course of 5 years), and the crime-reduction bene-fits are not reaped until many years after the intervention. However, it affects one form of crime immediately—child abuse by the parents in the targeted families. Recent surveys have indicated that about one in ten children are seriously abused or neglected by their parents (Carnegie Corporation, 1994). The rate is considerably higher among lower socioeconomic groups. The kind of early-childhood intervention considered here has been shown to reduce rates of child abuse by about 50 percent. Early home visits and day care would also produce considerable benefits by way of savings in the medical and social-service costs associated with foster care and should improve student performance in school.[1] Our estimates do not account for these benefits or for the savings to the criminal-justice system accruing from averted child abuse.

Once again, our estimates are only crude approximations of what the real costs and benefits are likely to be when we take into account start-up costs, economies of scale, and degradations in effectiveness when we shift from small pilot projects to large-scale public programs. They do not account for changes in criminal-justice-system costs and needs for services associated with lower rates of criminal activity on the parts of program participants.

In addition, the cost-effectiveness analysis presented here for the various early interventions is based on a static framework. For the current study, we have made the simplifying assumption that the population, age-specific crime rates, and all other factors affecting the overall crime rate do not change.[2] This assumption should not bias the results strongly in one direction or another. It must be understood, however, that such results from static analyses represent the per-capita effects of early intervention *on a single cohort.* Thus, we have answered the question, Which approaches are most cost-effective in reducing crime over the life of a cohort that is now young? We have not answered the question, Which approach will be most cost-effective at reducing crime across all cohorts over the next 20 years? All adult criminals are beyond the point of early intervention but are subject to the sanctions of the three-strikes law, so that law's benefits will be felt more broadly and quickly—but so will its costs. Thus, the form of the question may not sway the cost-effectiveness comparisons much.

---

[1]Barnett and Escobar (1990) estimate that crime reduction accounted for just 10 percent of the Perry Preschool enrichment and home-visit program's benefits. Other benefits included increased earnings, welfare reduction, and school cost savings.

[2]While the three-strikes analysis accounted for population growth, it also assumed that all other factors affecting the overall crime rate did not change.

Thus, within their scope of application, the policy implications of these findings are fairly clear. Based on current best estimates of program costs and benefits, investments in some interventions for high-risk youth may be several times more cost-effective in reducing serious crime than long mandatory sentences for repeat offenders. Furthermore, investments in these interventions may have additional payoffs that we do not account for in our cost-effectiveness estimates. For example, if such programs prove cost-effective, they could take some of the burden off our prisons and make the three-strikes law more affordable by diverting youth from a life of crime. In fact, our preliminary calculations suggest that a large share of the cost of some early-intervention alternatives may be offset by long-term reductions in prison costs (even after discounting).

Clearly, more information is needed on these promising alternatives. It would help considerably to have several pilot programs under way, with rigorous impact evaluations included. The sample sizes required for confident inference of results entail nontrivial commitments of public resources—more than is likely to be available from governmental or foundation sources for program development and testing purposes. The Orange County (California) Probation Department has been developing a program for their youngest delinquent youth, which they call the "8% Problem" (because 8 percent of their youths account for more than half of all repeat offenses by juveniles), but that program is in serious jeopardy because of the county's financial crisis. Of course, considering the potential cost-effectiveness of such programs, failure to find the funds for demonstration could be a case of penny-wise pound-foolishness.

Any effort designed to test parent training or delinquent supervision will also face concerns about the ethics of randomly assigning some youths to services and others to none. Regardless of existing evidence, many practitioners hold strong views regarding the benefits of particular interventions and prefer determining who is assigned to the limited slots on the basis of need or potential benefits, rather than random draw. Without much stronger public support, sounder knowledge may be prevented from developing because of these serious funding and research design issues.

Furthermore, convincing individuals to participate in social-assistance programs can be difficult, particularly if they perceive program involvement as stigmatizing. Since the interventions described here are targeted toward disadvantaged or underachieving youth, participation probably carries some negative connotations. Care must be taken to emphasize the positive side of the benefits arising from the interventions considered here, e.g., their potential to increase youth development, achievement, and self-confidence. However, the effects of stigmatization and program focus on outcomes certainly deserve further investigation.

One final impediment to formulating and testing early interventions for crime reduction is the lack of an obvious governmental authority with an interest in such approaches. California state agencies are divided into those charged with enforcing the law and implementing sanctions on the one hand and those charged with human-resource development and sustainment—education, public health, and welfare—on the other. Few people in the executive branch below the governor's office are likely to have a strong interest in applying tools familiar to the second set of agencies to achieve the goals of the first set. Of course, the tools are financed by all Californians and the goals are those of all Californians. But it may take an interagency consortium to effect the testing of the prevention approaches suggested here. Such a consortium might either have its own demonstration funds or be able to effect the transfer of funds from criminal-justice programs to carefully selected social programs, such as those described in this report, that serve criminal-justice purposes. Considering the multibillion-dollar annual budget of California's criminal-justice programs, an adequate diversion need entail only a tiny fraction of resources available. Activists interested primarily in social services and those interested primarily in crime prevention might find common cause in establishing an interagency consortium devoted to early intervention and assisting with its program.

SOME RESEARCH FINDINGS ON EARLY INTERVENTION

The tables below summarize the early-intervention research used in this report. This sample of the literature is neither exhaustive nor representative and was chosen based on availability and preexisting knowledge of the researchers.

Table A.1

Home Visits and Day Care

Author	Intervention Strategy and Cost	Outcome Measured	Treatment Effect
Lally, Mangione, and Honig, 1988	Weekly home visits and day care; cost unavailable	Processing as probation cases at 10-year follow-up	22% of controls vs. 6% of treatment group processed as probation cases
Olds et al., 1986a	Varying levels of prenatal and home visits; $2,180 per year per child	Reports of child abuse and neglect over 2 years	19% of controls vs. 4% of treatment group subject of child abuse report
Johnson and Walker, 1987	Biweekly home visits, classes, and day care; cost unavailable	Acting out and aggressive behavior scales	Significantly (p<.03) less acting out and aggression among treatment group
Larson, 1980	Home visits; cost unavailable	Infant accident rates	Accidents reduced by 50% among controls in year following intervention
Brooks-Gunn et al., 1993	Home visits, educational child care, and parent meetings; cost unavailable	Cognitive scores and behavioral problem scores	Significantly fewer behavior problems among treatment group
Schweinhart, Barnes, and Weikart, 1993	Two years enriched preschool, weekly home visits; approx. $7,500 per year per child	Arrests, education, and employment	2.3 lifetime arrests per person among treated group, 4.6 lifetime arrests per person among controls at age 27
Head Start, 1995	Enriched education and development, assisted access to health and social services (National program—strategy varies site to site); approx. $4,500 per year per child	Educational attainment, IQ, and school performance	Increased educational attainment and access to preventive health services

Table A.2

Parent Training

Author	Intervention Strategy and Cost	Outcome Measured	Treatment Effect
Patterson, Chamberlain, and Reid, 1982 *and*	Training parents to monitor and reward/punish children's behavior; cost unavailable	Stealing and antisocial behavior	Short-term reductions in deviant behaviors as observed in the home
Patterson, Reid, and Dishion, 1992			94% of controls vs. 50% of treatment group incarcerated at two-year follow-up
Barton et al., 1984	Functional family therapy— communication and negotiation; cost unavailable	Recidivism rates for delinquents	(1) 26% recidivism in treated group (base rate for district was 51%)
			(2) 60% of treated group and 93% of controls charged with committing an offense at 15 month follow-up
McCord et al. 1994	Assistance in family management and training in social skills; cost unavailable	School records and self-reports of delinquency	31% of treated group vs. 55% of controls reported a theft at one year follow-up
Hawkins, Von Cleve, and Catalano, 1991	Parent and teacher training; cost unavailable	Teacher ratings of aggressiveness and self-destructive behavior	Significant reduction in aggressiveness for white boys
Oregon Divorce Study (OSLC)	14 parent-training sessions for single mothers; $500 per family	Aggression, antisocial behavior, school failure	Study not yet completed

Table A.3

Graduation Incentives

Author	Intervention Strategy and Cost	Outcome Measured	Treatment Effect
Taggart, 1995	Cash and scholarship incentives; $3,130 per year per youth	Graduation rates and arrests	0.58 arrests per person for treated group vs. 0.17 arrests per person among controls over course of program

Table A.4

Delinquent Supervision

Author	Intervention Strategy and Cost	Outcome Measured	Treatment Effect
Andrews et. al., 1990	Meta-analysis of 80 program evaluations; cost unavailable	Recidivism	Meta-analysis found up to 50% reduction in recidivism among studies that found a measurable treatment effect
Lipsey, 1992	Behavioral, skill-oriented and multimodal intervention models; cost unavailable	Recidivism	Meta-analysis found a 10 to 20% reduction in recidivism among appropriate early delinquent programs
Orange County Probation Community Action 8% program, 1994	Intensive case management, mental health services, job counseling, and family supervision; approx. $10,000 per youth	Recidivism	Up to 50% reduction

DETAILED COST-EFFECTIVENESS RESULTS

This appendix provides the detailed derivation of this report's results. The plan of the appendix is first to review the key parameter estimates that determine the results and second to summarize the results, so that the objective of the derivations is clear. Then, finally, we will present the derivations in a series of overview equations and detailed calculation tables.

KEY PARAMETERS

The conclusions of this analysis are a consequence of the parameter estimates in Table B.1, which were obtained from the literature discussed in Chapter Three and in Table B.2. The first row of Table B.1 gives the proportion of the total youth cohort that each program can address. The smaller that proportion, the greater the targeting ratio (see row three of the table). Cost per program participant (row two) and the determinants of program effectiveness (rows four through seven) vary greatly across the programs.

RESULTS

The central results in this analysis are summarized in Tables B.3 and B.4. (These tables provide the plotting points for Figures 1, 2, and 3 in this report.) The results answer the report's three main questions:

- How cost-effective are early-intervention crime-prevention programs compared with California's three-strikes law that reduces crime by increasing prison sanctions?

Table B.1

Assumptions in the Analysis of Early-Intervention Programs

Assumption	Home Visit/ Day Care	Parent Training	Graduation Incentives	Delinquent Supervision
Percentage of cohort treatable by program	25	25	10	5
Cost per person treated (1993$)	29400	3000	12520	10000
Targeting ratio: crime per person in treatment group vs. that in population cohort	2	2	3	4.5
Pilot prevention rate: percentage of treatment-group crime prevented by treatment in pilot program	50	60	70	10
Modifiers of pilot prevention rate: Percentage decay due to scale-up	40	40	20	15
Additional % decay for juveniles	20	20	0	0
Additional % decay for adults	70	70	10	5

SOURCES: Costs per person treated and pilot program prevention rates from litera-ture sources discussed in Chapter Three. Targeting ratio for graduation incentives program from Table B.2. The smaller targeting ratios estimated for home visits and parent training reflect the broader reach of those very early interventions, and the greater targeting ratio for delinquent supervision reflects that program's focus on persons who have already started criminal careers. The modifiers that shrink the pilot program prevention rate, and the percentage of a youth cohort that is potentially treatable by a full-scale program, are rough estimates consistent with the targeting ratio and with the closeness of program intervention to the start of criminal careers.

Table B.2

Targeting Ratio for Graduation-Incentives Program

Item	Amount
Arrests per person during juvenile years in control group of QOP program	0.58
Juvenile arrests per year in California (000)	93.6
Size of California annual youth cohort (000)	481
Estimated arrests per person during juvenile years of California population	0.195
Targeting ratio of QOP program	2.97

SOURCES: Control group arrests in the graduation incentives program from the report on the Quantum Opportunity Program in Taggart (1995, p. 8). California juvenile crimes, in 1992, from Greenwood et al. (1994, Table D.5, p. 56). Size of California annual youth cohort (number of 0 to 17 year olds in 1993 divided by 18) from California Department of Finance, Demographic Research Unit.

Table B.3

Serious Crime Prevented per Million Program Dollars

| | California | Early-Intervention Program | | | |
Age of Offender	Three-Strikes Sanctions	Home Visit/ Day Care	Parent Training	Graduation Incentives	Delinquent Supervision
Juvenile	0	6	91	82	22
Adult	61	5	67	176	50
All ages	61	11	157	258	72

SOURCES: California three-strikes estimate from Greenwood et al. (1994, p. 18). Note that the three-strikes law only affects adults and so has no effect on juvenile crime. Early-intervention program estimates from Table B.13.

Table B.4

Criminal Justice System (CJS) Cost Savings ($ 000) per Million Program Dollars

Status of CJS Law	Home Visit/ Day Care	Parent Training	Graduation Incentives	Delinquent Supervision
Without three-strikes law	16	233	631	179
With three-strikes law fully implemented	27	397	1078	306

SOURCE: Table B.16.

Table B.5

Characteristics of a Full-Scale Program for an Annual Cohort: California

| | | Early Intervention Program | | | |
Item	California Three-Strikes Sanctions	Home Visit/ Day Care	Parent Training	Graduation Incentives	Delinquent Supervision
Percentage serious crime prevented	21.4	5.5	6.6	15.5	1.8
Annual program cost ($ million)	5520	3155	361	568	241
Cost ($ million) per 1% cut in crime	258	573	55	37	131

SOURCE: Estimates for early-intervention programs from Table B.17. Crime prevention by three strikes from Table B.18. Costs of three strikes from Greenwood et al. (1994, Table 4.2, p. 18).

- What savings in criminal-justice costs do the early-intervention programs generate?

- What proportion of overall crime would full-scale early-intervention programs prevent?

The results show that early intervention works best when it is neither too early nor too late. Neither home visits for babies nor counseling for children who are already delinquents work as well as providing training to parents of preteens or graduation incentives to teenagers. Both the graduation incentives and parent-training programs provide crime reductions per million program dollars substantially greater than those provided by the three-strikes program. Moreover, the cost offsets due to savings in criminal-justice costs from fewer criminal careers are also substantial for those two programs. Finally, full-scale implementation of those two early-intervention programs accomplish crime reductions that, if added together, equal that of the three-strikes law; at total cost that is 80 percent less than the cost of the three-strikes program.

COST-EFFECTIVENESS

This analysis measures program effectiveness by reductions in "serious" crime, as defined by California's Penal Code. About one-third of the FBI's index crimes are serious by this definition (see Table B.6). Tables B.7 and B.8 provide the information necessary to estimate the crime rates for the populations treated by the different

Table B.6

Index Crimes (000/year): California

Age of Offender	Serious Crime	Other Index Crime	Total Index Crime
Juvenile	293	567	860
Adult	995	1557	2552
All ages	1288	2124	3412

SOURCES: Greenwood et al. (1994, Table D.5, p. 56). Primary source was FBI's Uniform Crime Report for 1992, corrected for underreporting.

NOTES: "Serious crimes" are homicide, rape, robbery, assault, arson, and 60% of burglary, making "other index crimes" the remaining 40% of burglary, theft, and motor vehicle theft. The definitions are those in California's Penal Code.

Table B.7

Offender Status of Persons in Annual Cohort: California

Item	Non-Offenders	Low-Rate Offenders	High-Rate Offenders	All Offenders	Total Population
Number (000)	375	85	21	106	481
Distribution (%)	77.96	17.67	4.37	22.04	100.00

SOURCES: Size of California youth cohort estimated as 1/18th of the 8.653 million people in California who were 0 to 17 years old in 1993. Members of the 1993 cohort initiating a criminal career estimated from the analysis in Greenwood et al. (1994, Table E.1, p. 67).

Table B.8

Characteristics of Criminal Careers: California

Item	Low-Rate Offenders	High-Rate Offenders
Input Data		
Active adult offenders on street (000)	797	195
Annual initiations of adult criminal careers (000)	85	21
Serious crime per active adult offender-year	0.24	4.13
Derived estimates		
Adult street-years in criminal career[a]	9.38	9.29
Adult serious crimes per offender career[b]	2.25	38.35
Juvenile serious crimes per offender career[c]	0.66	11.29

SOURCES: Offenders in population, in 1993, from Greenwood et al. (1994, Table D.4, p. 55). Annual initiations from Table B.7. Annual offender crime rates from Greenwood et al. (1994, Table 4.1, p. 17).

[a]"Street-years" are the years that an offender is an active criminal (as opposed to having desisted, or to being incarcerated). They are estimated by dividing the offender population by annual initiations.

[b]Annual offense rate times street-years.

[c]Adult serious crimes in an offender career times the ratio of juvenile to adult serious crimes from Table B.6.

early-intervention programs (see Table B.9). Then, multiplying those crime rates by crime-prevention rates yields the crime prevented by each program (see Table B.10).

Table B.9

Crime Rates by Treatment Group

| | | Treatment Group | | | |
Type of Offender	General Population	Home Visit/ Day Care	Parent Training	Graduation Incentives	Delinquent Supervision
Distribution of Persons in Cohort by Offender Status (%)					
Nonoffender	77.96	55.93	55.93	33.89	0.83
Low-rate offender	17.67	35.34	35.34	53.01	79.52
High-rate offender	4.37	8.73	8.73	13.10	19.65
Total	100.00	100.00	100.00	100.00	100.00
Serious Crimes During Career of Average Person in Group					
Juvenile	0.61	1.22	1.22	1.83	2.75
Adult	2.07	4.14	4.14	6.22	9.32
Total	2.68	5.36	5.36	8.05	12.07

SOURCES: Tables B.1, B.7, and B.8.

NOTES: Percentages of low- and high-rate offenders in treatment groups equal the population percentages from Table B.7 times the targeting ratios from Table B.1. Multiplying the low- and high-rate offender percentages by the career crime rates from Table B.8 yields the estimated serious crimes during the career of the average person in a group.

Table B.10

Serious Crimes Prevented per Person Treated

Age of Offender	Home Visit/ Day Care	Parent Training	Graduation Incentives	Delinquent Supervision
Percentage of Treatment Group's Crime Prevented by Treatment				
Juveniles	24.0	28.8	56.0	8.5
Adults	7.2	8.6	50.4	8.1
Serious Crimes Prevented per Average Person Treated				
Juvenile	0.293	0.351	1.025	0.233
Adult	0.298	0.358	3.133	0.753
Total	0.591	0.709	4.158	0.986

SOURCES: Tables B.1 and B.9.

NOTES: Crime-prevention rates are the pilot program prevention rates from Table B.1 modified by the scale-up and juvenile and adult attenuation factors also in Table B.1. These factors account for full-scale programs rarely being as effective as small pilot programs, and for the tendency of program effects to decay with time since intervention. Multiplying the resultant effective prevention rates by the treatment group's number of career crimes per person, from Table B.9, gives the number of crimes prevented per program participant.

Finally, both program costs and crime-reduction benefits have to be discounted to the start of the intervention programs (see Tables B.11 and B.12) before being compared in Table B.13.

The following equation provides an overview of the estimated crimes prevented per program participant. The numerical examples present the calculation for the juvenile and adult portions of criminal careers as affected by the graduation-incentives program.

(Crimes over career per average person in population cohort)
x (targeting ratio)
x (prevention rate)
x (discount factor)
= NPV serious crimes prevented per program participant.

Graduation incentives, juvenile: $(0.61)(3)(0.560)(0.94) = 0.97$
Graduation incentives, adult: $(2.07)(3)(0.504)(0.66) = 2.08$.

The product of the first two factors in the equation (obtained from Tables B.9 and B.1) is the crimes per average person in the program cohort. Multiplying by the remaining factors (obtained from Tables B.10 and B.12) yields the number of those cohort crimes that are pre-

Table B.11

Discounted Program Cost per Participant

Cohort Year	Home Visit/ Day Care	Parent Training	Graduation Incentives	Delinquent Supervision
1	2700	3000	3130	10000
2	2700		3130	0
3	6000	0	3130	0
4	6000	0	3130	0
5	6000	0	0	0
6	6000	0	0	0
Sum	29400	3000	12520	10000
NPV	26238	3000	11816	10000

SOURCE: Table B.1, annual discount rate used to compute net present value is 4%.

NOTES: Home visit costs are spread approximately 10% in each of the first two cohort years and 20% in each of the following four years. Graduation-incentive costs are spread evenly over the four high-school years. Parent-training and delinquent-supervision program costs are all in the first cohort year.

Table B.12

Discounted Serious Crimes Prevented per Participant

Cohort Year	Home Visit/ Day Care	Parent Training	Graduation Incentives	Delinquent Supervision
	Serious Crimes Prevented by Cohort Year			
1	0.000	0.000	0.256	0.058
2	0.000	0.000	0.256	0.058
3	0.000	0.000	0.256	0.058
4	0.000	0.000	0.256	0.058
5	0.000	0.000	0.335	0.080
6	0.000	0.088	0.301	0.072
7	0.000	0.088	0.271	0.065
8	0.000	0.088	0.244	0.059
9	0.000	0.088	0.220	0.053
10	0.000	0.040	0.198	0.048
11	0.000	0.036	0.178	0.043
12	0.000	0.033	0.160	0.038
13	0.000	0.029	0.144	0.035
14	0.073	0.026	0.130	0.031
15	0.073	0.024	0.117	0.028
16	0.073	0.021	0.105	0.025
17	0.073	0.019	0.095	0.023
18	0.040	0.017	0.085	0.020
19	0.036	0.016	0.077	0.018
20	0.032	0.014	0.069	0.017
21	0.029	0.013	0.062	0.015
22	0.026	0.011	0.056	0.013
23	0.024	0.010	0.050	0.012
24	0.021	0.009	0.045	0.011
25	0.019	0.008	0.041	0.010
26	0.017	0.007	0.037	0.009
27	0.015	0.007	0.033	0.008
28	0.014	0.006	0.030	0.007
29	0.013	0.005	0.027	0.006
30	0.011	0.005	0.024	0.006
	Sum of Serious Crimes Prevented per Participant			
Juvenile	0.293	0.351	1.025	0.233
Adult	0.298	0.358	3.133	0.753
Total	0.591	0.709	4.158	0.986
	NPV of Serious Crimes Prevented per Participant			
Juvenile	0.166	0.273	0.967	0.220
Adult	0.129	0.200	2.077	0.499
Total	0.295	0.472	3.045	0.719

SOURCE: Table B.10; annual discount rate used to compute net present value is 4%.

NOTES: Juvenile crime spread evenly over participant ages 14 through 17. Adult crime spread over years from participant age 18 through cohort year 30, with a 10% per year desistance factor. Treatment starts at participant age 1 year for home visits, 9 years for parent training, and 14 years for the graduation incentives and delinquent-supervision programs.

Table B.13

Serious Crimes Prevented per Million Program Dollars

Item	Home Visit/ Day Care	Parent Training	Graduation Incentives	Delinquent Supervision
NPV Cost per Average Person Treated				
Cost (1993 $)	26238	3000	11816	10000
NPV Serious Crimes Prevented per Average Person Treated				
Juvenile serious crime	0.166	0.273	0.967	0.220
Adult serious crime	0.129	0.200	2.077	0.499
All serious crime	0.295	0.472	3.045	0.719
Serious Crime Prevented per Million Program Dollars				
Juvenile serious crime	6	91	82	22
Adult serious crime	5	67	176	50
All serious crime	11	157	258	72

SOURCES: Tables B.11 and B. 12.

NOTES: Discounted costs come from Table B.11. Discounted crime prevented comes from Table B.12.

vented by the program and then expresses that result as the present value as of the start of the intervention program.

The total serious crime prevented per average participant in the graduation-incentives program, 3.05, is the sum of the crimes prevented during the juvenile and adult years. Dividing that total by the $11,800 cost per participant (as of the start of the intervention, see Table B.11), produces the 258 serious crimes prevented per million program dollars that is reported in Table B.13.

CRIMINAL JUSTICE SYSTEM COST SAVINGS

By preventing some criminal careers, the early-intervention programs would save criminal-justice-system money. Fewer criminals would lead to fewer crimes, arrests, convictions, and imprisonment. Those reductions in criminal-justice system (CJS) activity generate cost savings that are offsets to the direct costs of the early-intervention programs.[1]

The model of the criminal-justice system developed for the analysis in Greenwood et al. (1994) depends on the realization that criminal-justice activity per adult[2] criminal career varies greatly with the offender (see Table B.14). Low- and high-rate offenders are defined in that analysis to divide the crime-rate distribution of imprisoned criminals in halves. The differential CJS activity leads to the differential CJS costs of criminal careers reported in Table B.15.

Table B.14

Adult Criminal Justice System Sanctions per Criminal Career: California

Sanction	Low-Rate Offender	High-Rate Offender	Average Offender
Without Three-Strikes Law			
Arrests	2.11	5.71	2.82
Years in jail	0.34	1.04	0.48
Years in prison	0.31	2.07	0.66
Total years incarcerated	0.64	3.11	1.13
With Three-Strikes Law Fully Implemented			
Arrests	2.07	4.21	2.50
Years in jail	0.33	0.82	0.43
Years in prison	0.53	4.91	1.40
Total years incarcerated	0.86	5.72	1.83

SOURCES: Runs of the California criminal justice model described in Greenwood et al. (1994). The model was run varying the number of low- and high-rate offenders starting adult criminal careers in year 1 of the 25-year simulation to find the CJS effects per low- and high-rate offender career.

---

[1]How those cost savings are used is a separate issue. They might be used to help pay for the early-intervention programs. Alternatively, they might be spent to increase the prison sentences for the criminals whose careers are not prevented by the early-intervention programs. The latter could happen if actual prison sentences served are currently being truncated due to prison congestion and would get longer if the inflow of new prisoners was reduced.

[2]The model in Greenwood et al. (1994) includes only the adult portion of criminal careers, because only adults are affected by California's three-strikes law. Consequently, our estimate of CJS cost savings from early-intervention programs is an underestimate due to the omission of savings in the juvenile-justice system.

Table B.15

Adult Criminal Justice System Costs per Criminal Career (1993 $)

Cost Component	Low-Rate Offender	High-Rate Offender	Average Offender
Without Three-Strikes Law			
Arrest and adjudication	4284	11713	5756
Jail	3384	10407	4776
Prison	7736	53583	16819
Total	15405	75703	27350
With Three-Strikes Law Fully Implemented			
Arrest and adjudication	4213	8733	5108
Jail	3348	8161	4301
Prison	14287	130441	37299
Total	21847	147335	46708

SOURCES: Runs of the California criminal justice model described in Greenwood et al. (1994). The model was run varying the number of low- and high-rate offenders starting adult criminal careers in year 1 of the 25-year simulation to find the CJS effects per low- and high-rate offender career.

NOTES: Costs in the analysis are in 1993 dollars, and the total CJS cost over a criminal career is given as the present value at the start of an adult criminal career using a 4% annual discount rate. Arrest and adjudication costs include police costs to accomplish the arrest and court costs (through trial if necessary) to process the arrest. Jail and prison costs include both operating and capital costs.

Applying these cost estimates to the number of low- and high-rate criminal careers prevented by early-intervention programs generates the cost-saving estimates in Table B.16.

The cost-savings calculation is summarized in the following equation. Once again, the numerical example is for the graduation-incentives program.

(Adult criminal careers prevented per million dollars)
x (CJS cost, $000, of an adult criminal career)
x (discount factor)
= NPV CJS cost savings ($000) per million program dollars.

Graduation incentives, low-rate offenders: (22.6)(15.4)(0.82) = 284
Graduation incentives, high-rate offenders: (5.6)(75.7)(0.82) = 347.

Table B.16

Adult Criminal-Justice System Cost Savings per Million Program Dollars

Item	Home Visit/ Day Care	Parent Training	Graduation Incentives	Delinquent Supervision
Adult Criminal Careers Prevented per Million Program Dollars				
Low-rate offender	0.97	10.18	22.61	6.42
High-rate offender	0.24	2.51	5.59	1.59
Total offenders	1.21	12.69	28.20	8.01
Adult CJS Costs ($ 000) Prevented per Million Program Dollars: NPV at Start of Adult Criminal Career				
Without three-strikes law	33	347	771	219
With three-strikes law	56	593	1317	374
Adult CJS Costs ($ Million) Prevented per Million Program Dollars: NPV at Start of Cohort Treatment				
Without three-strikes law	16	233	631	179
With three-strikes law	27	397	1078	306

SOURCES: Tables B.9, B.10, B.13, and B.15.

NOTES: The percentages of a cohort that are low- and high-rate offenders can be thought of as the numbers of low- and high-rate criminal careers prevented per person in a treatment cohort. Dividing by program cost per program participant, from Table B.13, gives criminal careers prevented per program dollar (top panel of table). Multiplying by CJS costs per criminal career, from Table B.15, gives CJS costs saved per program dollar, in present value as of the start of an adult criminal career (middle panel of table). Discounting those costs, respectively, to 18, 10, 5, and 5 years earlier expresses the cost savings as the present value as of the start of cohort treatment (bottom panel of table).

The total cost savings, $631,000 per million program dollars, is the sum of the savings from the low- and high-rate criminal careers prevented. Note that this is the CJS savings that the graduation-incentives program would generate without the three-strikes law. If the three-strikes law is fully implemented (thereby causing longer prison sentences and hence more prison costs per criminal career), then the CJS savings from the crime-prevention program would be even larger (see Table B.16).

FULL-SCALE PROGRAMS

It is possible for a crime-control program to be very cost-effective and yet still not be very useful in combating crime. This happens if the program, even at maximum size, can attack only a very small part of the crime problem. Tables B.17 and B.18 address this issue by showing what full-scale early-intervention programs could accomplish (Table B.17) and comparing it with what a fully implemented three-strikes program would accomplish (Table B.18).

The calculation of crime prevented by full-scale early-intervention programs is summarized in the following equation. The numerical example is for the graduation-incentives program.

(Annual cohort size)
x (proportion treatable by a full-scale program)
x (serious crimes in career)
x (prevention rate)
= serious crimes prevented annually by a full-scale program.

Graduation incentives, juvenile: $(481)(0.10)(1.83)(0.560) = 49$
Graduation incentives, adult: $(481)(0.10)(6.22)(0.504) = 151$.

The sources of the factors in this equation are, respectively, Tables B.7, B.1, B.9, and B.10. The total serious crime prevented in an annual youth cohort, 200, is the sum of that prevented in the juvenile and adult portions of criminal careers. This is a 15.5 percent reduction from the amount of crime the cohort would generate if there were no graduation incentives program (see Table B.17).

Table B.17

Characteristics of Full-Scale Program for an Annual Cohort: California

Item	General Population	Home Visit/ Day Care	Parent Training	Graduation Incentives	Delinquent Supervision
		Treatment Group			
	Size of Full-Scale Annual Cohort				
Cohort size (000)	481	120	120	48	24
	Serious Crimes from Career of Full-Scale Annual Cohort				
Juvenile serious crime (000)	293	147	147	88	66
Adult serious crime (000)	997	498	498	299	224
Total serious crime (000)	1290	645	645	387	290
% of serious crime in population	100.0	50.0	50.0	30.0	22.5
	Serious Crimes Prevented by Full-Scale Treatment of Annual Cohort				
Juvenile serious crime (000)	NA	35	42	49	6
Adult serious crime (000)	NA	36	43	151	18
Total serious crime (000)	NA	71	85	200	24
% of serious crime in population	NA	5.5	6.6	15.5	1.8
	Cost of Full-Scale Treatment of Annual Cohort				
Cost of treating cohort ($ million)	NA	3155	361	568	241
Cost ($ million) per 1% cut in crime	NA	573	55	37	131

SOURCES: Tables B.1, B.7, B.9, B.10, and B.11.

NOTES: Total cohort population in California, from Table B.7, times proportion treatable in a full-scale program, from Table B.1, gives the size of a full-scale program in California. Multiplying by serious crime in offender careers, from Table B.9, gives the crimes that would be committed by participants in a full-scale program if there were no treatment. Finally, multiplying by the prevention rates in Table B.10 yields the crimes prevented by a full-scale program. Dividing by the 1290 people in the total cohort converts the result into the proportion of crimes that would be prevented by a full-scale program. The cost per program participant, from Table B.11, times program size gives the cost of a full-scale program. Note that in this table program costs are discounted to the start of treatment, as usual in this analysis. The accounts of crimes from criminal careers, however, are not discounted. Rather, they are the undiscounted totals from cohort careers. This is not a problem because, since neither the total crime from the cohort nor the crime prevented by a program is discounted, the percentage reduction in crime achieved by the full-scale program is correctly estimated.

Table B.18

Serious Crime in California:
Annual Average (000), 1994–2018

Type of Offender	Previous Law	Three-Strikes Law	Change	Percentage Change
Juvenile	360	360	0	0.0
Adult	1219	881	−338	−27.7
Total	1579	1241	−338	−21.4

SOURCE: Greenwood et al. (1994).

NOTES: Reduction in adult serious crime from Greenwood et al. (1994, Table 4.2, p. 18). "Annual average" is the annualized value of 25 projection years using a 4% discount rate. Juvenile crime under previous law estimated from ratios of juvenile to adult crime from Greenwood et al. (1994, Table D.5, p. 56) allocated to California's definition of serious crime using Greenwood et al. (1994, Table B.1, p. 46). Juvenile crime under the three-strikes law is the same as under the previous law because three-strikes sanctions affect only adults.

Alexander, J. F., and B. V. Parsons, "Short Term Behavioral Intervention with Delinquent Families: Impact on Family Process and Recidivism," *Journal of Abnormal Psychology*, Vol. 81, No. 3, 1973, pp. 219–225.

Andrews, D. A., Ian Zinger, R. D. Hoge, James Bonta, Paul Gendreau, and Francis T. Cullen. "Does Correctional Treatment Work? A Clinically-Relevant and Psychologically-Informed Meta-Analysis," *Criminology*, Vol. 28, No. 3, 1990, pp. 369–404.

Barnett, W. Steven, and Colette M. Escobar, "Economic Costs and Benefits of Early Intervention," in Samuel J. Meisels and Jack P. Shonkoff, eds., *Handbook of Early Childhood Intervention*, New York: Cambridge University Press, 1990.

Barton, Cole, James F. Alexander, Holly Waldron, Charles W. Turner, and Janet Warburton, "General Treatment Effects of Functional Family Therapy: Three Replications," *American Journal of Family Therapy*, Vol. 13, No. 3, 1984, pp. 16–26.

Blumstein, Alfred, Jacqueline Cohen, Jeffrey A. Roth, and Christy A. Visher, eds., *Criminal Careers and "Career Criminals,"* Vol. II, National Research Council, National Academy of Sciences, Washington, D.C.: National Academy Press, 1986.

Brennan, Patricia A., Sarnoff A. Mednick, and Jan Volavka, "Biomedical Factors in Crime," in James Q. Wilson and Joan Petersilia, eds., *Crime*, San Francisco, Calif.: ICS Press, 1995.

Brooks-Gunn, Jeanne, Pam Kato Klebanov, Fong-ruey Liaw, and Donna Spiker, "Enhancing the Development of Low-Birthweight, Premature Infants: Changes in Cognition and Behavior over the First Three Years," *Child Development*, Vol. 64, 1993, pp. 736–753.

California Department of Corrections, *California Prisoners and Parolees, 1990*, Sacramento, Calif.: Youth and Adult Correctional Agency, 1991.

Carnegie Corporation of New York, *Starting Points: Meeting the Needs of Our Youngest Children*, The Report of the Carnegie Task Force on Meeting the Needs of Young Children, Waldorf, Md.: Carnegie Corporation of New York, 1994.

Currie, Janet, and Duncan Thomas, "Does Head Start Make a Difference?" *The American Economic Review*, Vol. 85, No. 3, June 1995, pp. 341–364.

Davidson, William S., L. Gottschalk, L. Gensheimer, and J. Mayer, *Interventions with Juvenile Delinquents: A Meta-analysis of Treatment Efficacy*, Washington, D.C.: National Institute of Juvenile Justice and Delinquency Prevention, 1984.

Davidson, William S., Robin Redner, Richard L. Amdur, and Christina M. Mitchell, *Alternative Treatments for Troubled Youth: The Case of Diversion from the Justice System*, New York: Plenum Press, 1990.

DeJong, William, *Preventing Interpersonal Violence Among Youth: An Introduction to School, Community and Mass Media Strategies*, Washington, D.C.: National Institute of Justice, NCJ #150484, 1994.

Ellickson, Phyllis L., and Robert M. Bell, *Prospects for Preventing Drug Use Among Young Adolescents*, Santa Monica, Calif.: RAND, R-3896-CHF, 1990.

Elliott, Delbert S., David Huizinga, and Scott Menard, *Multiple Problem Youth: Delinquency, Substance Use, and Mental Health Problems*, New York: Springer-Verlag, 1989.

Farrington, David P., "Early Developmental Prevention of Juvenile Delinquency," *Criminal Behaviour and Mental Health*, Vol. 4, England: Whurr Publishers, Ltd., 1994, pp. 209–227.

Garrett, Carol J., "Effects of Residential Treatment on Adjudicated Delinquents: A Meta-Analysis," *Journal of Research in Crime and Delinquency,* Vol. 22, No. 4, November 1985, pp. 287–308.

Gendreau, Paul, and Robert R. Ross, "Revivification of Rehabilitation: Evidence from the 1980s," *Justice Quarterly,* Vol. 4, No. 3, September 1987, pp. 349–407.

Gottfredson, Denise, "Changing School Structures to Benefit High-Risk Youth," Peter E. Leone, ed., *Understanding Troubled and Troubling Youth,* Newbury Park, Calif.: Peter E. Leone, 1990, pp. 246–271.

Greenwood, Peter, W., *Substance Abuse Problems Among High-Risk Youth and Potential Interventions,* Santa Monica, Calif.: RAND, RP-182, 1993.

Greenwood, Peter W., and Allan F. Abrahamse, *Selective Incapacitation,* Santa Monica, Calif.: RAND, R-2815-NIJ, 1982.

Greenwood, Peter W., C. Peter Rydell, Allan F. Abrahamse, Jonathan P. Caulkins, James Chiesa, Karyn E. Model, and Stephen P. Klein, *Three Strikes and You're Out: Estimated Benefits and Costs of California's New Mandatory-Sentencing Law,* Santa Monica, Calif.: RAND, MR-509-RC, 1994.

Greenwood, Peter W., and Franklin Zimring, *One More Chance: The Pursuit of Promising Intervention Strategies for Chronic Juvenile Offenders,* Santa Monica, Calif.: RAND, R-3214-OJJDP, May 1985.

Greenwood, Peter W., Albert J. Lipson, Allan F. Abrahamse, and Franklin Zimring, *Youth Crime and Juvenile Justice in California,* Santa Monica, Calif.: RAND, R-3016-CSA, 1983.

Hahn, Andrew, Tom Leavitt, and Paul Aaron, *Evaluation of the Quantum Opportunities Program (QOP): Did the Program Work? A Report on the Postsecondary Outcomes and Cost-Effectiveness of the QOP Program (1989–1993),* Waltham, Mass.: Brandeis University, 1994.

Hawkins, J. David, Elizabeth Von Cleve, and Richard F. Catalano, Jr., "Reducing Early Childhood Aggression: Results of a Primary Prevention Program, *Journal of the American Academy of Child and Adolescent Psychiatry,* Vol. 30, No 2, March 1991, pp. 208–217.

Head Start Bureau, *Head Start Information Kit, 1995,* Washington D.C.: U.S. Department of Health and Human Services, United States Government Printing Office, 1995.

Johnson, Dale L., and Todd Walker, "Primary Prevention of Behavior Problems in Mexican-American Children," *American Journal of Community Psychology,* Vol. 15, No. 4, 1987, pp. 375–385.

Keeler, Emmett B., and Shan Cretin, "Discounting of Life-Saving and Other Nonmonetary Effects," *Management Science,* Vol. 29, No. 3, 1983, pp. 300–306.

Kumpfer, Karol L, and Charles W. Turner, "The Social Ecology Model of Adolescent Substance Abuse: Implications for Prevention," *The International Journal of the Addictions,* Vol. 25, 1990–1991, pp. 435–463.

Lally, J. Ronald, Peter L. Mangione, and Alice S. Honig, "The Syracuse University Family Development Research Program: Long-Range Impact on an Early Intervention with Low-Income Children and Their Families," D. R. Powell, ed., *Parent Education as Early Childhood Intervention,* Norwood, N.J.: Ablex, 1988, pp. 79–104.

Larson, Charles P., "Efficacy of Prenatal and Postpartum Home Visits on Child Health and Development," *Pediatrics,* Vol. 66, No. 2, August 1980, pp. 191–197.

Lipsey, Mark W., "Juvenile Delinquency Treatment: A Meta-Analytic Inquiry into the Variability of Effects," Thomas Cook et al., eds., *Meta-Analysis for Explanation,* New York: Russell Sage Foundation, 1992, pp. 83–126.

Lipton, Douglas, Robert Martinson, and Judith Wilks, *The Effectiveness of Correctional Treatment: A Survey of Treatment Evaluation Studies,* New York: Praeger, 1975.

Loeber, R., and M. LeBlanc, "Toward a Developmental Criminology," M. Tonry and N. Morris, eds., *Crime and Justice,* Vol. 12, Chicago: University of Chicago Press, 1990, pp. 375–473.

Loeber, Rolf, and Magda Stouthamer-Loeber, "Family Factors as Correlates and Predictors of Juvenile Conduct Problems and Delinquency," Michael Tonry and Norval Morris, eds., *Crime and*

Justice: An Annual Review of Research, Vol. 7, Chicago: University of Chicago Press, 1986, pp. 29–149.

McCord, Joan, Richard E. Tremblay, Frank Vitaro, and Lyse Desmarais-Gervais, "Boys' Disruptive Behaviour, School Adjustment, and Delinquency: The Montreal Prevention Experiment," *International Journal of Behavioral Development*, Vol. 17, No. 0, 1994, pp. 1–14.

National Research Council, *Understanding Child Abuse and Neglect*, Washington, D.C.: National Academy Press, 1993.

Olds, David L., Charles R. Henderson, Jr., Robert Chamberlin, and Robert Tatelbaum, "Preventing Child Abuse and Neglect: A Randomized Trial of Nurse Home Visitation," *Pediatrics*, Vol. 78, No. 1, July 1986a, pp. 65–78.

Olds, D. L., C. R. Henderson, R. Tatelbaum, and R. Chamberlain, "Improving the Delivery of Prenatal Care and a Randomized Trial of Nurse Home Visitation," *Pediatrics*, Vol. 77, 1986b, pp. 16–28.

Orange County Probation Department, *The "8% Problem": Chronic Juvenile Offender Recidivism*, Orange County, Calif.: Orange County Probation Department Publications, March 1994.

Palmer, Ted, *Correctional Intervention and Research: Current Issues and Future Prospects*, Lexington, Mass.: Lexington Books, D.C. Heath and Co., 1978.

Patterson, G. R., P. Chamberlain, and J. B. Reid, "A Comparative Evaluation of a Parent Training Programme," *Behavior Therapy*, Vol. 13, 1982, pp. 638–650.

Patterson, G. R., J. B. Reid, and T. J. Dishion, *Antisocial Boys*, Eugene, Oreg.: Castalra, 1992.

Pentz, Mary Ann, James Dwyer, David MacKinnon, Brian Flay, William Hanse, Eric Wang, and C. Anderson Johnson, "A Multi-community Trial for Primary Prevention of Adolescent Drug Abuse: Effects on Drug Prevalence," *Journal of the American Medical Association*, Vol. 261, 1989, pp. 3259–3266.

Raine, Adrian, Patricia Brennan, and Sarnoff A. Mednick, "Birth Complications Combined with Early Maternal Rejection at Age

One Year Predispose to Violent Crime at Age 18 Years," *Annals of Journal of General Psychiatry*, Vol. 51, December 1994, pp. 984–988.

Reiss, A. J., Jr., and J. A. Roth, eds., *Understanding and Preventing Violence*, Washington, D.C.: National Academy Press, 1993.

Ross, R. R., E. Fabiano, E. A. Ewles, and C. D. Ewles. "Reasoning and Rehabilitation," *International Journal of Offender Therapy and Comparative Criminology*, Vol. 32, 1988, pp. 29–35.

Ross, Robert R., and Paul Gendreau, *Effective Correctional Treatment*, Toronto, Canada: Butterworths, 1980.

Ross, R. R., and B. D. Ross, "Delinquency Prevention Through Cognitive Training," *Educational Horizons*, Vol. 67, No. 4, 1989, pp. 124–130.

Rydell, C. Peter, and Susan S. Everingham, *Controlling Cocaine: Supply Versus Demand Programs*, Santa Monica, Calif.: RAND, MR-331-ONDCP/A/DPRC, CA. 1994.

Sampson, Robert J., "The Community," in James Q. Wilson and Joan Petersilia, eds., *Crime*, San Francisco, Calif.: ICS Press, 1995, pp. 193–216.

Schweinhart, L. J., H. V. Barnes, and D. P. Weikart, *Significant Benefits*, Ypsilanti, Mich.: High/Scope, 1993.

Sechrest, Lee, Susan O. White, and Elizabeth D. Brown, eds., *The Rehabilitation of Criminal Offenders: Problems and Prospects*, Washington, D.C.: National Academy of Sciences, 1979.

Seitz, Victoria, "Intervention Programs for Impoverished Children: A Comparison of Educational and Family Support Models," *Annals of Child Development*, Vol. 7, London: Jessica Kingsley Publishers, Ltd., 1990, pp. 73–103.

Taggart, Robert, *Quantum Opportunity Program*, Philadelphia: Opportunities Industrialization Centers of America, 1995.

Thornberry, Terence P., "Toward an Interactional Theory of Delinquency," *Criminology*, Vol. 25, 1987, pp. 863–891.

Tolan, Patrick, and Nancy Guerra, *What Works in Reducing Adolescent Violence: An Empirical Review of the Field*, Center for the Study and Prevention of Violence, Colo.: University of Colorado, July 1994.

Tremblay, Richard E., Joan McCord, Helene Boileau, Pierre Charlebois, Claude Gagnon, Marc Le Blanc, and Serge Larivee, "Can Disruptive Boys Be Helped to Become Competent?" *Psychiatry*, Vol. 54, May 1991, pp. 148–161.

U.S. Department of Education, *Digest of Education Statistics, 1994*, Washington, D.C.: U.S. Government Printing Office, 1994.

U.S. Department of Justice, *Crime Victimization in the United States, 1991*, A National Crime Victimization Survey Report, Washington, D.C.: Office of Justice Programs, Bureau of Justice Statistics, NCJ-139563, 1992.

Widom, Cathy Spatz, *The Cycle of Violence*, NIJ Research in Brief, Washington, D.C.: National Institute of Justice, NCJ 136607, October 1992.

Wolfgang, Marvin, R. M. Figlio, and T. Sellin, *Delinquency in a Birth Cohort*, Chicago: University of Chicago Press, 1972.

Wolfgang, Marvin, and Paul E. Tracy, *The 1945 and 1958 Birth Cohorts: A Comparison of the Prevalence, Incidence and Severity of Delinquent Behavior*, Philadelphia, Pa.: Center for Studies in Criminology and Criminal Law, University of Pennsylvania, 1982.

Yoshikawa, Hirokazu, "Prevention as Cumulative Protection: Effects of Early Family Support and Education on Chronic Delinquency and Its Risks," *Psychological Bulletin*, Vol. 115, No 1, 1994. pp. 1–26.

Zimring, Franklin, and Gordon Hawkins, *Incapacitation: Penal Confinement and the Restraint of Crime*, New York: Oxford University Press, 1995.